Any book which you borrow remains your responsibility until the loan slip
is cancelled

Tobacco consumption in various countries

Edited by P. N. Lee
Statistician, Tobacco Research Council

Compiled by M. J. Wilson, *Tobacco Research Council*

RESEARCH PAPER 6, *4th edition*
TOBACCO RESEARCH COUNCIL : LONDON 1975

Published by
Tobacco Research Council
Glen House, Stag Place, London SWIE 5AG

Designed and produced by
Ruari McLean Associates, Dollar, Scotland

Printed and bound in Great Britain by
T. & A. Constable Ltd, Edinburgh

ISBN 0 901026 07 7

Introduction

The fourth edition of Research Paper No. 6 brings up to date the information about total tobacco consumption in various countries which was published in the third edition in 1972. In preparing a fourth edition of the Research Paper, the opportunity has been taken to revise, where appropriate, certain figures in the light of more recent information which has become available. In addition, the geographical coverage of the report has been extended and statistics of tobacco consumption during the last ten years or so are now presented for a number of Central and South American, African and Asian countries not included in previous editions.

Cigarette and cigar consumption are shown both in numbers and in pounds weight. Where the numbers of cigarettes consumed were not available, the cigarette consumption in millions has been calculated from the consumption in pounds weight, for each country, by using a standard conversion factor of 2·205 lbs. per 1,000 except where otherwise stated. For cigars and cigarillos, various conversion factors have been used according to the proportion of cigarillos and the type of cigars smoked in each country.

Before making an international comparison of the estimates of the number of manufactured cigarettes consumed per adult per annum, it is recommended that care should be taken to notice any factors that may bias such a simple comparison. For example, in Switzerland an appreciable volume of tobacco goods is consumed by foreign visitors. In some other countries, notably in Norway and to a lesser extent in Australia, Canada and New Zealand, hand-rolled cigarettes form an appreciable proportion of total cigarette consumption.

The population figures have been obtained either from the publications of the United Nations and the World Health Organisation or from official sources in the country of origin.

The Tobacco Research Council is grateful to British-American Tobacco Co. Ltd and their Associated Companies overseas for providing much of the up-dated information and all of the information relating to new territories which has been published in this Research Paper. Other figures have been provided by Government Departments and by the tobacco trade in the various countries concerned and the Council is grateful for the continued co-operation of these organisations in making their statistics of tobacco consumption available for publication.

P. N. Lee

Consumption per adult in each country

	Consumption per adult per annum (a)							
	Manufactured cigarettes (b)				All tobacco goods			
	1935 Number	1950	1965	1973	1935 Lbs.	1950	1965	1973
Argentina	1,060(c)	1,460	1,660	1,940	4·5(c)	4·7	4·5	4·9
Australia	450(d)	1,280(d)	2,680(d)	3,080(d)	3·9(d)	6·3(d)	7·4(d)	7·5(d)
Austria	860	1,100	1,930	2,550	3·8	3·2	4·8	5·9
Barbados	...	...	1,110	1,620	...	...	2·6	3·7
Belgium	790	1,240	1,980	2,730	7·0	6·2	7·7	8·5
Brazil	600(e)	1,140	1,220	1,490	5·5(e)	5·7	4·6	4·5
Canada	700	1,790	3,310	3,450	4·9	7·6	10·1	10·0
Chile	...	...	1,220	1,320	...	...	2·5	2·5
Costa Rica	...	...	1,850	2,060	...	...	3·8	3·5
Denmark	470	1,290	1,500	1,850	6·5	8·1	8·2	8·0
El Salvador	...	...	750	1,020	...	...	3·7	3·3
Finland	1,350	1,640	1,920	2,040	2·7	3·6	4·5	5·2
France	530	930	1,510	1,920	3·8	4·1	5·2	5·9
Germany	720(f)	—	—	—	4·8(f)	—	—	—
West Germany	—	630	2,100	2,610	—	4·1	6·2	6·8
Ghana	...	...	480	480	...	...	1·1	1·3
Greece	960	1,600	1,930	2,550	2·4	4·0	4·9	6·3
Hong Kong	...	...	3,310	2,780	...	...	6·9	5·5
Iceland	480	1,490	1,840	2,030	2·7	4·9	6·5	7·5
India	80(g)	100	180	170	1·9(g)	2·1	1·8	1·4
Indonesia	...	...	...	230(h)	...	...	...	1·8(h)
Ireland	1,210	2,510	2,690	3,340	4·5	6·9	6·6	6·8
Italy	450(i)	660(j)	1,540	1,930	1·9(i)	2·0(j)	3·7	4·4
Jamaica	...	...	1,270(k)	1,350(k)	...	...	2·9(k)	3·0(k)
Japan	880(f)	1,220(f)	2,350(f)	3,240(f)	3·0(f)	3·1(f)	5·2(f)	7·2(f)
Kenya	...	...	390(h)	470(h)	...	...	0·8(h)	0·9(h)
Malawi	...	...	150	200	...	...	0·3	0·5
Malaysia	...	...	1,440	1,600	...	...	3·1	3·4
Mauritius	...	...	1,610(h)	1,920(h)	...	...	2·8(h)	3·3(h)
Mexico	1,440	1,510	1,510	1,360	3·2	3·4	3·4	3·0
Morocco	240	510	570	690(l)	0·9	1·4	1·6	1·8(l)
Netherlands	680	1,120	2,020	2,370	8·4	7·5	9·3	9·8
New Zealand	530	1,420	2,280	2,510	4·5	7·2	7·6	7·1
Nicaragua	...	...	1,140	1,520	...	...	2·3	2·7
Norway	300	510	520	640	3·2	4·3	4·7	5·2

Consumption per adult per annum (a)

	Manufactured cigarettes (b)				*All tobacco goods*			
	1935 Number	1950	1965	1973	1935 Lbs.	1950	1965	1973
Pakistan	...	...	450(f)	760(f)	...	...	3·7(f)	3·8(f)
Portugal	270(c)	620	1,130	1,490(l)	1·4(c)	1·9	·2·7	3·4(l)
Sierra Leone	...	...	280(h)	430(h)	...	...	1·5(h)	1·3(h)
Singapore	...	...	2,380	2,490	...	...	6·0	6·3
South Africa	520	1,170	1,080	1,380	3·2	4·9	4·6	5·1
Spain	390	430	1,760	2,260	3·5	3·1	4·5	5·6
Sweden	380	810	1,360	1,580	3·6	4·1	4·7	4·0
Switzerland	540(m)	1,500	3,050	3,370	4·7(m)	6·0	9·0	9·4
Turkey	960	1,220	1,820	2,050(l)	2·7	3·1	4·4	4·8(l)
United Kingdom	1,590	2,180	2,680	3,230	4·8	5·7	6·1	6·2
U.S.A.	1,450	3,240	3,800	3,850	7·8	10·1	10·7	9·2
Venezuela	...	...	1,900(h)	2,210(h)	...	...	...	...

Notes

(a) The consumption per adult per annum figures in the above table are based on the total sales of tobacco goods and the population aged 15 years and over resident in each country. In some countries, notably Switzerland, the consumption per adult statistics are exaggerated due to the appreciable volume of sales to borderers, tourists and seasonal workers (see note (d) on page 77).

(b) The tobacco used in hand-rolled cigarettes made by the smoker is included in 'All tobacco goods'. Hand-rolled cigarettes form an appreciable proportion of total cigarettes in Australia, Canada, New Zealand and Norway. Estimates, by trade or other sources, of the weight and number of hand-rolled cigarettes consumed in these countries during 1973 along with figures for cigarette consumption per adult per annum adjusted to include hand-rolled cigarettes are as follows:

Country	Tobacco for hand-rolled cigarettes	Estimated cigarette equivalent	Consumption per adult per annum of manufactured and hand-rolled cigarettes
	Mn. lbs.	Millions	Number
Australia	7·3	3,292	3,440
Canada	16·2	6,723	3,870
New Zealand	1·4	548	2,760
Norway	8·4	3,470	1,830

(c) Figures are for year 1940.
(d) Figures refer to the year ended 30th June.
(e) Annual average 1935–1939.
(f) Figures refer to the year ended 31st March.
(g) Figures are for year 1948.
(h) Figures refer to the year ended 30th September.
(i) Annual average year ended 30th June, 1931 – year ended 30th June, 1935.
(j) Annual average year ended 30th June, 1946 – year ended 30th June, 1950.
(k) Figures based on population aged 14 years and over.
(l) Figures are for year 1972.
(m) Annual average 1934–1937.

Symbols used in the Tables

...	Data not available
—	Nil
0·0	Magnitude less than half of unit employed
*	Estimate

I. Argentina

Calendar year	Cigarettes Millions	Cigarettes Mn. lbs.	Cigars Millions	Cigars Mn. lbs.	Cigarillos Millions	Cigarillos Mn. lbs.	Smoking tobacco Mn. lbs.	Snuff Mn. lbs.	Total Mn. lbs.	Population Total Mns.	Population 15 + Mns.	Consumption per adult Cigarettes Number	Consumption per adult Total Lbs.
1940	10,422	28·7	480	6·6	Combined with cigars		8·8	0·0	44·1	14·2	9·8*	1,060	4·5
1941	10,383	28·6	490	6·9			8·9	0·0	44·4	14·4	10·0*	1,040	4·4
1942	10,991	30·3	502	7·1			8·8	0·0	46·2	14·6	10·1*	1,090	4·6
1943	11,011	30·3	471	4·6			9·4	0·0	44·3	14·9	10·3*	1,070	4·3
1944	11,929	32·9	507	4·7			9·1	0·0	46·7	15·1	10·5*	1,140	4·4
1945	12,893	31·1	495	10·2			8·6	0·0	49·9	15·4	10·7*	1,200	4·7
1946	13,921	35·5	434	5·0	Millions Mn. lbs.		7·9	0·0	48·4	15·7	10·8*	1,290	4·5
1947	15,249	38·9	437	4·9	8	0·0	7·6	0·0	51·4	15·9	11·0	1,390	4·7
1948	16,389	41·8	313	4·1	15	0·0	7·6	0·0	53·5	16·3	11·5*	1,430	4·7
1949	17,797	44·8	317	4·0	9	0·0	8·2	0·0	57·0	16·7	11·7	1,520	4·9
1950	17,520	43·4	293	3·1	9	0·0	9·5	0·0	56·0	17·2	12·0	1,460	4·7
1951	17,792	44·3	284	2·9	6	0·0	9·6	0·3	57·1	17·4	12·2	1,460	4·7
1952	19,360	47·5	341	3·6	7	0·0	10·4	0·0	61·5	17·6	12·3	1,570	5·0
1953	19,840	47·8	291	3·9	6	0·0	8·7	0·0	60·4	17·8	12·5	1,590	4·8
1954	19,498	47·3	296	3·1	5	0·0	8·7	0·0	59·1	18·0	12·6	1,550	4·7
1955	20,942	50·0	224	2·8	32	0·1	7·0	0·0	59·9	18·3	12·8	1,640	4·7
1956	21,367	51·0	234	2·6	27	0·1	8·4	0·0	62·1	18·7	13·1	1,630	4·7
1957	21,934	51·3	230	2·1	41	0·2	7·0	0·0	60·6	19·0	13·3	1,650	4·6
1958	22,369	53·7	201	2·2	18	0·1	7·1	0·0	63·1	19·4	13·6	1,640	4·6
1959	23,332	53·4	179	1·9	20	0·1	7·8	0·0	63·2	19·8	13·7	1,700	4·6
1960	20,818	51·6	164	1·6	23	0·1	8·7	0·0	62·0	20·0	14·0	1,490	4·4
1961	23,109	55·4	264	2·6	83	0·4	8·3	0·0	66·7	20·3	14·2	1,630	4·7
1962	23,489	54·1	170	1·7	100	0·5	8·1	0·0	64·4	20·6	14·4	1,630	4·5
1963	23,698	54·7	120	1·2	100	0·5	8·3	0·0	64·7	21·0	14·7	1,610	4·4
1964	25,125	57·1	150	1·5	60	0·3	8·1	0·0	67·0	21·2	14·9	1,690	4·5

Argentina (contd)

Calendar year	Cigarettes		Cigars		Cigarillos		Smoking tobacco	Snuff	Total	Population		Consumption per adult	
												Cigarettes	Total
	Millions	Mn. lbs.	Millions	Mn. lbs.	Millions	Mn. lbs.	Mn. lbs.	Mn. lbs.	Mn. lbs.	Total Mns.	15+ Mns.	Number	Lbs.
1965	25,105	58·0	160	1·6	40	0·2	7·9	0·0	67·7	21·6	15·1	1,660	4·5
1966	24,200	55·9	160	1·6	40	0·2	8·7	0·0	66·4	21·9	15·4	1,570	4·3
1967	24,783	56·9	130	1·3	40	0·2	8·2	0·0	66·6	22·3	15·6	1,590	4·3
1968	26,188	60·2	120	1·2	40	0·2	7·5	0·0	69·1	22·6	15·8	1,660	4·4
1969	27,569	64·2	120	1·2	40	0·2	7·3	0·0	72·9	22·9	16·1	1,710	4·5
1970	29,357	65·4	100	1·0	40	0·2	7·8	0·0	74·4	23·3	16·3	1,800	4·6
1971	30,286	68·1	80	0·8	38	0·2	7·5	0·0	76·6	23·7	16·6	1,820	4·6
1972	31,911	72·9	60	0·6	38	0·2	7·5	0·0	81·2	24·1	16·9	1,890	4·8
1973	33,398	76·4	50	0·5	38	0·2	7·2	0·0	84·3	24·6	17·2	1,940	4·9

Notes

(a) Details of the quantities of tobacco products consumed were obtained from the following sources:

1940–57 *Panorama Tabacalero Argentino*. Ministry of Commerce and Industry.

1958–66 The numbers and weight of cigarettes, cigars and cigarillos and the weight of other manufactured tobacco consumed were provided by the Secretary of Industry and Commerce, Buenos Aires.

1967–73 The numbers and weight of cigarettes and the weight of smoking tobacco consumed were obtained from trade sources. The figures for cigars and cigarillos are based on information issued by the Secretariat of Agriculture.

(b) The population figures are estimates based on a report by the National Institute of Statistics and Census following the census of population in 1970.

2. Australia

Year ended 30th June	Cigarettes		Cigars		Tobacco for hand-rolled cigarettes and pipe	Total	Population		Consumption per adult	
	Millions	Mn. lbs.	Millions	Mn. lbs.	Mn. lbs.	Mn. lbs.	Total Mns.	15+ Mns.	Cigarettes Number	Total Lbs.
1920	2,204	4·9	64	0·7	11·6	17·2	5·4	3·6*	610	4·8
1921	2,376	5·2	58	0·6	10·6	16·4	5·4	3·7	640	4·4
1922	2,267	5·0	53	0·6	12·6	18·2	5·6*	3·8*	600	4·8
1923	2,124	4·7	54	0·6	12·5	17·8	5·7*	3·9*	540	4·6
1924	2,286	5·0	50	0·5	13·0	18·5	5·8*	4·0*	570	4·6
1925	2,372	5·2	54	0·6	13·3	19·1	5·9	4·1*	580	4·7
1926	2,542	5·6	50	0·5	13·7	19·8	6·0*	4·2*	610	4·7
1927	2,706	6·0	51	0·5	13·8	20·3	6·1*	4·3*	630	4·7
1928	2,851	6·3	48	0·5	13·8	20·6	6·2*	4·4*	650	4·7
1929	2,890	6·4	44	0·4	14·1	20·9	6·3*	4·6*	640	4·6
1930	2,783	6·1	44	0·4	14·4	20·9	6·5	4·6*	610	4·5
1931	2,079	4·6	39	0·3	13·5	18·4	6·5*	4·7*	440	3·9
1932	1,858	4·1	23	0·2	13·6	17·9	6·6	4·7*	400	3·8
1933	2,040	4·5	25	0·2	13·8	18·5	6·6	4·8	430	3·9
1934	2,072	4·6	29	0·3	13·9	18·8	6·7	4·9*	420	3·8
1935	2,189	4·8	30	0·3	14·1	19·2	6·7	4·9*	450	3·9
1936	2,417	5·3	26	0·2	14·7	20·2	6·8	5·0*	480	4·0
1937	2,630	5·8	31	0·3	15·0	21·1	6·8	5·1	520	4·1
1938	2,869	6·3	33	0·3	15·6	22·2	6·9	5·2	550	4·3
1939	3,180	7·0	33	0·3	15·8	23·1	7·0	5·2	610	4·4
1940	3,384	7·5	27	0·2	16·1	23·8	7·0	5·3	640	4·5
1941	3,154	6·9	31	0·2	15·5	22·6	7·1	5·4	580	4·2
1942	3,585	7·9	35	0·3	16·8	25·0	7·2	5·5	650	4·5
1943	3,619	8·0	22	0·2	17·5	25·7	7·2	5·5*	660	4·6
1944	3,627	8·0	17	0·1	16·7	24·8	7·3	5·5*	660	4·5

Australia (contd)

Year ended 30th June	Cigarettes		Cigars		Tobacco for hand-rolled cigarettes and pipe	Total	Population		Consumption per adult	
	Millions	Mn. lbs.	Millions	Mn. lbs.	Mn. lbs.	Total Mn. lbs.	Total Mns.	15+ Mns.	Cigarettes Number	Total Lbs.
1945	3,370	7.4	15	0.1	15.2	22.7	7.4	5.6	600	4.1
1946	3,618	7.9	15	0.1	16.6	24.6	7.5	5.6*	650	4.4
1947	4,424	9.6	16	0.2	19.4	29.2	7.6	5.7	780	5.1
1948	5,575	12.3	20	0.2	19.7	32.2	7.7	5.7*	980	5.6
1949	6,555	14.7	22	0.2	19.2	34.1	7.9	5.8*	1,130	5.9
1950	7,665	17.3	25	0.2	20.3	37.8	8.2	6.0*	1,280	6.3
1951	9,219	20.9	28	0.2	21.3	42.4	8.4	6.1	1,510	7.0
1952	9,420	21.4	29	0.2	21.3	42.9	8.6	6.3	1,500	6.8
1953	8,976	20.0	21	0.2	22.6	42.8	8.8	6.3	1,420	6.8
1954	10,487	23.1	25	0.2	22.6	45.9	9.0	6.4	1,640	7.2
1955	11,515	25.5	25	0.2	21.2	46.9	9.2	6.5	1,770	7.2
1956	12,616	27.7	27	0.2	19.3	47.2	9.4	6.7	1,880	7.0
1957	13,878	30.5	26	0.2	19.0	49.7	9.6	6.8	2,040	7.3
1958	14,699	32.5	32	0.2	18.3	51.0	9.8	6.9	2,130	7.4
1959	15,677	35.3	34	0.2	16.8	52.3	10.1	7.0	2,240	7.5
1960	17,101	39.3	38	0.2	16.1	55.6	10.3	7.0	2,440	7.9
1961	18,044	41.7	45	0.3	15.2	57.2	10.5	7.2	2,510	7.9
1962	18,824	43.3	60	0.3	13.7	57.3	10.7	7.5	2,510	7.6
1963	19,649	45.2	68	0.3	12.5	58.0	10.9	7.7	2,550	7.5
1964	20,572	47.2	84	0.4	11.5	59.1	11.1	7.8	2,640	7.6
1965	21,400	48.6	87	0.4	10.4	59.4	11.3	8.0	2,680	7.4
1966	22,644	49.9	83	0.4	9.9	60.2	11.6	8.2	2,760	7.3
1967	22,247	48.8	84	0.4	9.3	58.5	11.8	8.4	2,650	7.0
1968	23,667	51.8	93	0.5	9.3	61.6	12.0	8.5	2,780	7.2
1969	24,883	54.3	105	0.5	9.2	64.0	12.3	8.7	2,860	7.4
1970	25,938	55.5	118	0.5	9.1	65.1	12.5	8.9	2,910	7.3
1971	26,331	56.9	117	0.5	8.9	66.3	12.8	9.1	2,900	7.3
1972	27,321	58.2	133	0.6	9.4	68.2	13.0	9.2	2,950	7.4
1973	28,998	60.8	163	0.6	8.9	70.3	13.1	9.4	3,080	7.5

Notes

(a) Details of the weight of tobacco consumed by products were obtained from the Commonwealth Bureau of Census and Statistics, Canberra and from trade sources.

(b) Factors for conversion from weight to count for cigarettes and cigars were obtained from H.M. Customs and trade sources.

3. Austria

Calendar year	Cigarettes		Cigars		Cigarette tobacco	Pipe tobacco	Chewing tobacco	Snuff	Total	Population		Consumption per adult	
	Millions	Mn. lbs.	Millions	Mn. lbs.	Mn. lbs.	Mn. lbs.	Mn. lbs.	Mn. lbs.	Mn. lbs.	Total Mns.	15+ Mns.	Cigarettes Number	Total Lbs.
1923	2,935	7.0	158	1.6	3.7	8.7	0.5	0.3	21.8	6.5	4.9*	600	4.4
1924	3,741	8.5	205	2.0	3.1	8.8	0.6	0.3	23.3	6.6*	4.9*	760	4.8
1925	3,973	8.9	216	2.1	3.0	8.6	0.7	0.3	23.6	6.6	4.9*	810	4.8
1926	4,395	9.8	204	2.0	2.9	8.5	0.7	0.3	24.2	6.6*	5.0*	880	4.8
1927	4,512	10.0	201	1.9	3.1	7.9	0.8	0.3	24.0	6.6*	5.0*	900	4.8
1928	4,800	10.5	209	2.0	3.2	7.5	0.9	0.3	24.4	6.7*	5.1*	940	4.8
1929	4,925	10.5	207	2.0	3.4	7.1	0.9	0.3	24.2	6.7*	5.1*	970	4.7
1930	4,809	10.3	206	2.0	3.5	7.0	0.8	0.3	23.9	6.7	5.1*	940	4.7
1931	4,940	10.6	175	1.7	2.6	6.9	0.8	0.3	22.9	6.7*	5.1*	970	4.5
1932	5,512	11.4	144	1.4	1.6	6.6	0.8	0.2	22.0	6.7	5.1*	1,080	4.3
1933	5,102	10.7	122	1.2	1.4	6.7	0.8	0.2	21.0	6.7	5.1*	1,000	4.1
1934	4,658	9.8	107	1.0	1.6	7.1	0.7	0.2	20.4	6.8	5.2	900	3.9
1935	4,452	9.4	104	1.0	1.9	6.8	0.6	0.2	19.9	6.8	5.2*	860	3.8
1936	4,332	9.2	106	1.0	2.4	6.8	0.6	0.2	20.2	6.8	5.3	820	3.8
1937	4,211	8.9	103	1.0	2.4	6.7	0.6	0.2	19.8	6.8	5.3	790	3.7
1938	5,004	10.6	129	1.2	2.6	6.5	0.6	0.2	21.7	6.8	5.3	940	4.1
1939	6,395	14.1	157	1.4	2.6	6.3	0.5	0.1	25.0	6.7	5.3	1,210	4.7
1940	7,810	17.2	175	1.5	3.1	6.6	0.7	0.2	29.3	6.7	5.3*	1,470	5.5
1941	9,249	20.4	176	1.6	3.7	7.7	0.9	0.2	34.5	6.7	5.3*	1,750	6.5
1942	8,561	18.9	147	1.3	3.4	7.3	0.8	0.1	31.8	6.8	5.3*	1,620	6.0
1943	8,168	18.0	121	1.1	4.1	5.4	0.7	0.1	29.4	6.8	5.3*	1,540	5.5
1944	6,510	14.4	94	0.8	3.2	4.5	0.3	0.1	23.2	6.8	5.3*	1,230	4.4
1945	2,554	5.6	37	0.3	1.2	1.0	0.1	0.0	8.2	6.8	5.3*	480	1.5
1946	2,244	4.9	62	0.5	0.1	0.5	0.1	0.0	6.1	7.0	5.5*	410	1.1
1947	3,136	6.3	57	0.6	0.0	0.5	0.1	0.0	7.5	6.9	5.4*	580	1.4
1948	3,923	8.5	72	0.8	0.0	0.9	0.1	0.1	10.4	7.0	5.4*	730	1.9
1949	4,781	10.5	60	0.7	0.0	2.8	0.2	0.1	14.3	6.9	5.4*	890	2.6

Austria (contd)

Calendar year	Cigarettes		Cigars		Cigarette tobacco	Pipe tobacco	Chewing tobacco	Snuff	Total	Population		Consumption per adult	
	Millions	Mn. lbs.	Millions	Mn. lbs.	Mn. lbs.	Mn. lbs.	Mn. lbs.	Mn. lbs.	Total Mn. lbs.	Total Mns.	15 + Mns.	Cigarettes Number	Total Lbs.
1950	5,953	13·1	58	0·6	0·2	3·0	0·3	0·1	17·3	6·9	5·4*	1,100	3·2
1951	6,609	14·6	66	0·7	0·3	2·9	0·3	0·1	18·9	6·9	5·3	1,250	3·6
1952	6,913	15·2	72	0·7	0·4	2·6	0·2	0·1	19·2	6·9	5·4	1,280	3·6
1953	7,132	15·7	76	0·7	0·4	2·5	0·2	0·0	19·5	7·0	5·4*	1,320	3·6
1954	6,329	14·0	77	0·7	0·4	2·3	0·2	0·0	17·6	7·0	5·4*	1,170	3·3
1955	7,144	15·8	85	0·8	0·4	2·2	0·2	0·0	19·4	7·0	5·4	1,320	3·6
1956	7,918	17·5	89	0·9	0·4	2·0	0·2	0·0	21·0	7·0	5·5	1,440	3·8
1957	8,349	18·4	94	0·8	0·4	1·9	0·1	0·0	21·6	7·0	5·5	1,520	3·9
1958	8,899	19·4	98	0·8	0·4	1·8	0·1	0·0	22·5	7·0	5·5	1,620	4·1
1959	9,295	20·3	98	0·8	0·4	1·7	0·1	0·0	23·3	7·0	5·5	1,690	4·2
1960	9,451	20·9	96	0·8	0·4	1·6	0·1	0·0	23·8	7·1	5·5	1,720	4·3
1961	9,284	21·2	101	0·8	0·4	1·6	0·1	0·0	24·1	7·1	5·5	1,690	4·4
1962	9,719	21·4	103	1·3	0·4	1·5	0·1	0·0	24·7	7·1	5·5	1,770	4·5
1963	10,101	22·3	91	1·0	0·4	1·4	0·1	0·0	25·2	7·2	5·5	1,840	4·6
1964	10,436	23·0	86	0·9	0·4	1·4	0·1	0·0	25·8	7·2	5·6	1,860	4·6
1965	10,827	23·9	85	0·9	0·4	1·3	0·1	0·0	26·6	7·3	5·6	1,930	4·8
1966	11,507	25·4	83	0·9	0·4	1·4	0·1	0·0	28·2	7·3	5·6	2,050	5·0
1967	11,771	26·0	82	0·9	0·4	1·4	0·1	0·0	28·8	7·3	5·6	2,100	5·1
1968	11,982	26·5	80	0·9	0·4	1·3	0·0	0·0	29·1	7·3	5·6	2,140	5·2
1969	12,379	27·4	84	0·9	0·3	1·1	0·0	0·0	29·7	7·4	5·6	2,210	5·3
1970	13,037	28·8	80	0·9	0·3	1·0	0·0	0·0	31·0	7·4	5·6	2,330	5·5
1971	13,603	30·0	77	0·9	0·2	0·9	0·0	0·0	32·1	7·5	5·6	2,410	5·7
1972	13,451	29·7	69	0·9	0·2	0·7	0·0	0·0	31·5	7·5	5·7	2,370	5·6
1973	14,499	32·0	68	0·8	0·2	0·7	0·0	0·0	33·7	7·5	5·7	2,550	5·9

Notes

Details of the numbers and weight of cigarettes and cigars and of the weight of other manufactured tobacco products consumed were either provided by the Austrian Tobacco Monopoly or obtained from the annual reports of the Monopoly.

4. Barbados

Calendar year	Cigarettes		Cigars and cigarillos		Smoking tobacco	Snuff	Total	Population		Consumption per adult	
	Millions	Mn. lbs.	Millions	Mn. lbs.	Mn. lbs.	Mn. lbs.	Total Mn. lbs.	Total Mns.	15 + Mns.	Cigarettes Number	Total Lbs.
1964	185	0·41	0	0·00	0·01	0·01	0·43	0·24	0·15	1,250	2·9
1965	167	0·37	0	0·00	0·01	0·01	0·39	0·25	0·15	1,110	2·6
1966	158	0·35	0	0·00	0·01	0·01	0·37	0·25	0·15	1,030	2·4
1967	176	0·39	0	0·00	0·01	0·01	0·41	0·25	0·16	1,120	2·6
1968	185	0·41	0	0·00	0·01	0·01	0·43	0·25	0·16	1,160	2·7
1969	154	0·34	0	0·01	0·01	0·01	0·36	0·25	0·16	940	2·2
1970	181	0·40	0	0·01	0·02	0·01	0·43	0·24	0·16	1,150	2·7
1971	154	0·34	0	0·01	0·01	0·01	0·36	0·24	0·16	960	2·3
1972	181	0·40	0	0·01	0·01	0·01	0·43	0·24	0·16	1,130	2·7
1973	267	0·59	0	0·01	0·01	0·00	0·61	0·25	0·17	1,620	3·7

Notes

(a) Details of numbers of cigarettes, cigars and cigarillos and of the weight of smoking tobacco and snuff consumed were obtained from *Overseas Trade Report*, published by the Barbados Government Statistical Services.

(b) Cigarette consumption in pounds weight has been estimated from the number of cigarettes consumed by using a conversion factor of 2·205 lbs. per 1,000. The conversion factor used for cigars and cigarillos was 6·615 lbs. per 1,000.

(c) Population Figures have been extracted from the publication *Abstract of Statistics*.

5. Belgium

Calendar year	Cigarettes		Cigars		Cigarillos		Other manufactured tobacco	Total	Population		Consumption per adult	
	Millions	Mn. lbs.	Millions	Mn. lbs.	Millions	Mn. lbs.	Mn. lbs.	Total Mn. lbs.	Total Mns.	15 + Mns.	Cigarettes Number	Total Lbs.
1921	3,421	7·5	240	2·5	192	1·1	25·6	36·7	7·6*	5·7*	600	6·4
1922	3,546	7·8	297	3·1	210	1·2	27·8	39·9	7·6*	5·7*	620	7·0
1923	3,775	8·3	314	3·3	252	1·4	28·6	41·6	7·7*	5·8*	650	7·2
1924	4,155	9·2	301	3·2	259	1·4	28·6	42·4	7·7*	5·8*	720	7·3
1925	4,207	9·3	277	2·9	301	1·7	28·4	42·3	7·8	5·9*	710	7·2
1926	4,457	9·8	235	2·5	262	1·4	29·3	43·0	7·8*	5·9*	760	7·3
1927	4,829	10·6	274	2·9	279	1·5	29·1	44·1	7·9*	6·0*	800	7·4
1928	5,540	12·2	275	2·9	286	1·6	28·3	45·0	7·9*	6·1*	910	7·4
1929	6,108	13·5	289	3·0	331	1·8	27·8	46·1	8·0*	6·1*	1,000	7·6
1930	6,799	15·0	283	3·0	347	1·9	27·5	47·4	8·1	6·2	1,100	7·6
1931	6,838	15·1	275	2·9	334	1·8	28·0	47·8	8·1*	6·2*	1,100	7·7
1932	5,982	13·2	228	2·4	321	1·8	28·0	45·4	8·2	6·3*	950	7·2
1933	5,525	12·2	203	2·1	357	2·0	27·5	43·8	8·2	6·3*	880	7·0
1934	4,981	11·0	178	1·9	412	2·3	28·2	43·4	8·3	6·3*	790	6·9
1935	4,955	10·9	193	2·0	511	2·8	28·5	44·2	8·3	6·3	790	7·0
1936	5,116	11·3	197	2·1	580	3·2	29·4	46·0	8·3	6·4*	800	7·2
1937	5,258	11·6	192	2·0	584	3·2	28·5	45·3	8·3	6·5*	810	7·0
1938	5,108	11·3	194	2·0	615	3·4	29·1	45·8	8·4	6·5	790	7·0
1939	5,128	11·3	179	1·9	556	3·1	31·6	47·9	8·4	6·5*	790	7·4
1940†	4,150	9·2	175	1·8	429	2·4	25·5	38·9	8·3	6·5*	640	6·0
1941	3,723	8·2	140	1·5	243	1·3	23·4	34·4	8·3	6·5	570	5·3
1942	3,284	7·2	105	1·1	218	1·2	19·3	28·8	8·2	6·5*	510	4·4
1943	1,889	4·2	101	1·1	208	1·1	9·7	16·1	8·2	6·5*	290	2·5
1944	2,070	4·6	75	0·8	181	1·0	8·7	15·1	8·3	6·5*	320	2·3
1945	2,563	5·7	107	1·1	250	1·4	13·4	21·6	8·3	6·6	390	3·3
1946	6,386	14·1	125	1·3	302	1·7	22·3	39·4	8·4	6·6*	970	6·0
1947	8,549	18·9	94	1·0	238	1·3	21·7	42·9	8·5	6·7	1,280	6·4
1948	8,901	19·6	87	0·9	260	1·4	21·7	43·6	8·6	6·8*	1,310	6·4
1949	8,414	18·6	85	0·9	261	1·4	22·0	42·9	8·6	6·8	1,240	6·3

† Period from 1st January to 31st July, 1940 only.

Belgium (contd)

Calendar year	Cigarettes Millions	Cigarettes Mn. lbs.	Cigars Millions	Cigars Mn. lbs.	Cigarillos Millions	Cigarillos Mn. lbs.	Other manufactured tobacco Mn. lbs.	Total Mn. lbs.	Population Total Mns.	Population 15+ Mns.	Consumption per adult Cigarettes Number	Consumption per adult Total Lbs.
1950	8,399	18·5	83	0·9	261	1·4	21·6	42·4	8·6	6·8	1,240	6·2
1951	8,197	18·1	91	1·0	285	1·6	21·3	42·0	8·7	6·9	1,190	6·1
1952	8,115	17·9	123	1·3	385	2·1	23·1	44·4	8·8	6·9	1,180	6·4
1953	8,217	18·1	131	1·4	445	2·5	22·1	44·1	8·8	6·9	1,190	6·4
1954	8,263	18·2	149	1·6	510	2·8	21·7	44·3	8·8	6·9	1,200	6·4
1955	8,652	19·1	158	1·7	537	3·0	20·9	44·7	8·9	6·9	1,250	6·5
1956	9,132	20·1	173	1·8	577	3·2	20·5	45·6	8·9	6·9	1,320	6·6
1957	9,859	21·7	190	2·0	595	3·3	20·0	47·0	9·0	7·0	1,410	6·7
1958	10,480	23·1	193	2·0	561	3·1	19·5	47·7	9·1	7·0	1,500	6·8
1959	10,308	22·7	217	2·3	597	3·3	19·3	47·6	9·1	7·0	1,470	6·8
1960	10,973	24·2	232	2·4	647	3·6	18·5	48·7	9·2	7·0	1,570	7·0
1961	11,253	24·8	257	2·7	661	3·6	18·1	49·2	9·2	7·0	1,610	7·0
1962	11,868	26·2	282	3·0	732	4·0	17·6	50·8	9·2	7·0	1,700	7·3
1963	12,325	27·2	267	2·8	681	3·8	16·6	50·4	9·3	7·0	1,760	7·2
1964	12,791	28·2	303	3·2	829	4·6	16·1	52·1	9·4	7·1	1,800	7·3
1965	14,083	31·1	317	3·3	814	4·5	15·5	54·4	9·4	7·1	1,980	7·7
1966	15,147	33·4	316	3·3	730	4·0	14·6	55·3	9·6	7·3	2,070	7·6
1967	15,448	34·1	299	3·1	746	4·1	14·8	56·1	9·6	7·3	2,120	7·7
1968	15,814	34·9	284	3·0	801	4·4	14·5	56·8	9·6	7·3	2,170	7·8
1969	16,633	36·7	285	3·0	790	4·4	13·2	57·3	9·7	7·4	2,250	7·7
1970	17,632	38·9	265	2·8	749	4·1	11·9	57·7	9·7	7·4	2,380	7·8
1971	18,334	40·4	285	3·0	859	4·7	11·4	59·5	9·7*	7·4*	2,480	8·0
1972	19,165	42·3	295	3·1	891	4·9	10·8	61·1	9·7*	7·4*	2,590	8·3
1973	20,236	44·6	301	3·2	845	4·7	10·3	62·8	9·7*	7·4*	2,730	8·5

Notes

(a) Details of the numbers of cigarettes, cigars and cigarillos and of the weight of other manufactured tobacco consumed were provided by the National Institute of Statistics of Belgium, Brussels, for the years up to 1950. The figures for 1951 onwards were obtained from trade sources and confirmed by the Belgian Federation of Tobacco Producers.

(b) Cigarette consumption in pounds weight has been estimated from the number of cigarettes consumed by using a conversion factor of 2·205 lbs. per 1,000. The conversion factors used for cigars and cigarillos were 10·5 lbs. per 1,000 and 5·51 lbs. per 1,000 respectively.

6. Brazil

Calendar year	Cigarettes		Cigars		Cut tobacco	Plug tobacco	Total	Population		Consumption per adult	
	Millions	Mn. lbs.	Millions	Mn. lbs.	Mn. lbs.	Mn. lbs.	Total Mn. lbs.	Total Mns.	15+ Mns.	Cigarettes Number	Total Lbs.
1935/39 (Average)	13,411	29·6	180	2·8	2·8	85·8	121·0	38·6	22·2*	600	5·5
1940/44 (Average)	20,688	45·6	158	2·4	2·6	89·0	139·6	43·1	24·8*	830	5·6
1945	21,637	47·7	158	2·4	2·5*	90·2	142·8	46·2	26·7*	810	5·3
1946	24,229	53·4	175	2·7	2·5*	90·6	149·2	47·3	27·4*	880	5·4
1947	27,360	60·3	159	2·4	2·5	90·8	156·0	48·4	28·1*	970	5·6
1948	29,460	64·7	133	2·0	2·5	91·0	160·2	49·6	28·8*	1,020	5·6
1949	32,500	71·7	130	2·0	2·5*	91·1	167·3	50·8	29·5*	1,100	5·7
1950	34,640	76·4	160	2·4	2·4*	91·2	172·4	52·0	30·3	1,140	5·7
1951	36,500	80·5	225	3·4	2·3*	91·4	177·6	53·2	30·9*	1,180	5·7
1952	40,400	89·1	192	2·9	2·3*	91·6	185·9	54·5	31·5*	1,280	5·9
1953	41,600	91·7	200	3·1	2·3*	91·7	188·8	55·8	32·1*	1,300	5·9
1954	42,000	92·6	196	3·0	2·0*	91·7	189·3	57·1	32·8*	1,280	5·8
1955	45,426	100·2	252	3·9	1·9	91·6	197·6	60·2	34·4*	1,320	5·7
1956	46,632	102·8	237	3·7	2·0	91·4	199·9	62·0	35·4*	1,320	5·6
1957	48,664	107·3	352	5·5	2·0	91·2	206·0	63·8	36·3*	1,340	5·7
1958	53,868	118·8	332	5·1	2·5	90·8	217·2	65·7	37·3*	1,440	5·8
1959	56,289	124·1	307	4·8	2·7	90·4	222·0	68·0	38·5	1,460	5·8

Brazil (contd)

Calendar year	Cigarettes Millions	Cigarettes Mn. lbs.	Cigars Millions	Cigars Mn. lbs.	Cigarillos Millions	Cigarillos Mn. lbs.	Cut tobacco Mn. lbs.	Plug tobacco Mn. lbs.	Pipe tobacco Mn. lbs.	Total Mn. lbs.	Population Total Mns.	Population 15+ Mns.	Consumption per adult Cigarettes Number	Consumption per adult Total Lbs.
1960	56,657	124·9	292	4·5	—	—	2·9	89·8	0·0	222·1	71·0	40·7	1,390	5·5
1961	58,950	130·0	280	4·3	—	—	3·1	88·1	0·1	225·6	73·2	42·0	1,400	5·4
1962	60,573	133·6	270	4·2	—	—	3·3	86·4	0·1	227·6	75·3	43·3	1,400	5·3
1963	60,782	134·0	260	4·0	—	—	3·5	84·6	0·1	226·2	77·4	44·6	1,360	5·1
1964	59,216	130·6	250	3·9	44	0·2	3·7	82·8	0·1	221·3	79·7	46·0	1,290	4·8
1965	57,952	127·8	240	3·7	45	0·2	4·0	81·0	0·1	216·8	82·0	47·4	1,220	4·6
1966	61,566	135·8	210	3·3	42	0·2	3·5	79·1	0·2	222·1	84·3	48·8	1,260	4·6
1967	64,346	141·9	180	2·8	39	0·2	3·7	77·2	0·2	226·0	86·8	50·4	1,280	4·5
1968	68,733	151·5	131	2·0	46	0·2	3·8	75·3	0·2	233·0	89·3	51·9	1,320	4·5
1969	70,280	154·9	114	1·7	52	0·3	3·9	73·3	0·2	234·3	91·9	53·5	1,310	4·4
1970	72,731	160·3	94	1·5	60	0·3	4·1	71·3	0·2	237·7	94·5	55·1	1,320	4·3
1971	75,819	167·2	83	1·3	59	0·3	4·1	69·1	0·2	242·2	97·2	56·8	1,330	4·3
1972	82,722	182·4	79	1·2	56	0·2	4·2	66·9	0·2	255·1	100·0	58·5	1,410	4·4
1973	89,617	197·6	72	1·1	66	0·3	4·9	64·6	0·2	268·7	102·9	60·3	1,490	4·5

Notes

(a) Details of the quantities of tobacco products consumed were obtained from the following sources:
1935–54 *Foreign Agriculture Report*, August, 1949 and March, 1955, United States Department of Agriculture, Washington.
1955–58 *Producao Industrial Brasileira*, 1958 and *Annuario Estatistico do Brasil*, 1961. Conselho Nacional de Estatistica.

(b) Since 1958 no official Government statistics for the tobacco industry have been available. The figures shown above for these years are estimates from trade sources.

(c) Cigarette consumption in pounds weight has been estimated from the number of cigarettes consumed by using a conversion factor of 2·205 lbs. per 1,000. The conversion factors used for cigars and cigarillos were 15·5 lbs. per 1,000 and 449 lbs. per 1,000 respectively.

(d) Plug tobacco is consumed mainly in the rural communities and consists of dark air-cured tobacco which is delivered by farmers to local markets where it is sold by weight for use in hand-rolled cigarettes, pipe smoking and chewing.

(e) The details of the numbers and weights of cigars prior to 1957 are of uncertain accuracy.

(f) For the years 1960–73 the total population figures have been extracted from the publication *Annuario Estatistico do Brasil*.

17

7. Canada

Calendar year	Cigarettes Millions	Cigarettes Mn. lbs.	Cigars Millions	Cigars Mn. lbs.	Tobacco for hand-rolled cigarettes and pipe Mn. lbs.	Plug tobacco Mn. lbs.	Snuff Mn. lbs.	Total Mn. lbs.	Population Total Mns.	Population 15+ Mns.	Consumption per adult Cigarettes Number	Consumption per adult Total Lbs.
1920	2,441	5·9	270	3·4	14·1	6·6	0·7	30·7	8·7*	5·7*	430	5·4
1921	2,440	5·9	214	2·7	12·9	6·2	0·7	28·4	8·8	5·8	420	4·9
1922	2,043	4·9	179	2·2	11·3	10·1	0·7	29·2	9·0*	5·9*	350	4·9
1923	2,291	5·5	193	2·4	11·1	9·1	0·8	28·9	9·1*	6·0*	380	4·8
1924	2,515	6·0	169	2·1	11·3	8·3	0·8	28·5	9·2*	6·1*	410	4·7
1925	2,823	6·8	177	2·2	12·2	8·5	0·8	30·5	9·3	6·2*	460	4·9
1926	3,227	7·7	177	2·2	12·8	8·0	0·8	31·5	9·5	6·3*	510	5·0
1927	3,781	9·1	178	2·2	13·2	7·7	0·9	33·1	9·6	6·5*	580	5·1
1928	4,436	10·6	187	2·3	15·3	7·1	1·0	36·3	9·8	6·6*	670	5·5
1929	5,081	12·2	199	2·5	14·5	6·5	1·0	36·7	10·0	6·8*	750	5·4
1930	5,036	12·1	183	2·3	15·5	5·9	1·0	36·8	10·2	7·0*	720	5·3
1931	4,533	10·9	152	1·9	16·5	5·3	0·9	35·5	10·4	7·1	640	5·0
1932	3,713	8·9	133	1·7	17·3	4·6	0·8	33·3	10·5	7·2*	520	4·6
1933	4,317	10·4	115	1·4	17·3	4·2	0·7	34·0	10·6	7·4*	580	4·6
1934	4,822	11·6	120	1·5	18·0	4·2	0·8	36·1	10·7	7·5*	640	4·8
1935	5,305	12·7	125	1·6	18·3	3·9	0·8	37·3	10·8	7·6*	700	4·9
1936	5,600	13·4	122	1·5	19·2	3·7	0·8	38·6	11·0	7·7*	730	5·0
1937	6,698	16·1	130	1·6	20·9	3·6	0·8	43·0	11·0	7·8*	860	5·5
1938	6,872	16·5	132	1·7	21·3	3·2	0·8	43·5	11·2	7·9*	870	5·5
1939	7,126	17·1	133	1·7	23·7	3·2	0·8	46·5	11·3	8·0*	890	5·8
1940	7,572	18·2	166	2·1	25·5	3·1	0·8	49·7	11·4	8·2*	920	6·1
1941	8,582	20·6	191	2·4	25·0	3·0	0·9	51·9	11·5	8·3	1,030	6·3
1942	10,240	24·6	201	2·5	24·8	3·5	0·9	56·3	11·7	8·4*	1,220	6·7
1943	11,257	27·0	196	2·5	23·8	3·5	0·9	57·7	11·8	8·5*	1,320	6·8
1944	11,666	28·0	198	2·5	23·1	3·2	1·0	57·8	11·9	8·6*	1,360	6·7
1945	14,265	34·2	207	2·6	25·3	3·2	1·0	66·3	12·1	8·6*	1,660	7·7
1946	14,867	35·7	221	2·8	25·6	2·9	1·0	68·0	12·3	8·8*	1,690	7·7
1947	15,143	36·3	216	2·7	24·9	2·7	1·0	67·6	12·6	8·9*	1,700	7·6
1948	15,853	38·0	210	2·6	25·9	2·3	1·0	69·8	12·8	9·1*	1,740	7·7
1949	16,836	40·4	209	2·6	25·2	2·5	1·0	71·7	13·4	9·5	1,770	7·5

Canada (contd)

Calendar year	Cigarettes Millions	Cigarettes Mn. lbs.	Cigars Millions	Cigars Mn. lbs.	Tobacco for hand-rolled cigarettes and pipe Mn. lbs.	Plug tobacco Mn. lbs.	Snuff Mn. lbs.	Total Mn. lbs.	Population Total Mns.	Population 15+ Mns.	Consumption per adult Cigarettes Number	Consumption per adult Total Lbs.
1950	17,172	41·2	199	2·5	25·9	2·3	0·9	72·8	13·7	9·6	1,790	7·6
1951	15,672	37·6	169	2·1	27·3	2·0	0·9	69·9	14·0	9·8	1,600	7·1
1952	17,844	42·8	200	2·5	31·0	1·8	0·9	79·0	14·5	10·0	1,780	7·9
1953	21,000	50·4	235	2·9	26·1	1·8	0·8	82·0	14·8	10·2	2,060	8·0
1954	22,116	53·1	245	3·1	24·5	1·5	0·9	83·1	15·3	10·4*	2,130	8·0
1955	24,576	59·0	253	3·2	23·6	1·5	0·8	88·1	15·7	10·6	2,320	8·3
1956	27,000	64·8	256	3·2	21·2	1·2	0·8	91·2	16·1	10·9	2,480	8·4
1957	30,144	72·3	293	3·7	20·8	1·1	0·8	98·7	16·6	11·1	2,720	8·9
1958	32,404	77·8	323	4·0	21·8	1·3	0·8	105·7	17·0	11·4	2,840	9·3
1959	33,822	81·2	311	3·9	22·5	1·2	0·8	109·6	17·4	11·6	2,920	9·4
1960	34,289	82·3	332	4·2	22·7	1·1	0·9	111·2	17·8	11·8	2,910	9·4
1961	36,699	88·1	337	4·2	22·9	1·1	0·8	117·1	18·2	12·0	3,060	9·8
1962	38,683	92·8	352	4·4	23·3	1·1	0·9	122·5	18·6	12·3	3,140	10·0
1963	39,877	95·7	387	4·8	22·3	1·0	0·8	124·6	18·9	12·5	3,190	10·0
1964	40,639	97·5	491	4·9	21·2	1·0	0·9	125·5	19·2	12·8	3,170	9·8
1965	43,013	103·2	489	4·9	22·0	0·9	0·9	131·9	19·6	13·0	3,310	10·1
1966	46,276	111·1	437	4·4	19·2	0·9	0·8	136·4	19·9	13·4	3,450	10·2
1967	46,864	112·5	445	4·4	18·0	0·8	0·8	136·5	20·4	13·7	3,420	10·0
1968	46,269	111·0	462	4·6	19·3	0·7	0·8	136·4	20·7	14·1	3,280	9·7
1969	46,582	111·8	509	5·1	19·0	0·6	0·8	137·3	21·1	14·4	3,230	9·5
1970	49,823	119·6	560	5·6	19·1	0·6	0·8	145·7	21·4	14·9	3,340	9·8
1971	50,864	122·1	624	6·2	19·6	0·6	0·8	149·3	21·7	15·3	3,320	9·8
1972	53,291	127·9	570	5·7	19·2	0·6	0·8	154·2	21·8	15·5	3,440	9·9
1973	54,863	131·7	609	6·1	19·7	0·6	0·8	158·9	22·1	15·9	3,450	10·0

Notes

(a) Details of the quantities of tobacco products consumed were obtained from the following sources:

1920–48 *Historical Series of Tobacco Statistics*, Agricultural Division, Dominion Bureau of Statistics, Ottawa, 1950.

1949–57 *Canadian Statistical Review*, Dominion Bureau of Statistics, Ottawa, 1957 and 1958.

1958–67 *Tobacco and Tobacco Products Statistics Quarterly* formerly *Quarterly Stocks and Consumption of Unmanufactured Tobacco*, Industry Division, Dominion Bureau of Statistics.

1968–73 *Production and Disposition of Tobacco Products*, Manufacturing and Primary Industries Division, Statistics Canada (formerly known as Dominion Bureau of Statistics).

(b) Cigarette consumption in pounds weight was estimated from the number of cigarettes consumed by using a conversion factor of 2·4 lbs. per 1,000. The conversion factor used for cigars was 12·5 lbs. per 1,000 for the years up to and including 1963, thereafter a figure of 10 lbs. per 1,000 was used.

(c) The sources of the population figures were as follows:

1920–24 *The Canadian Year-Book*. 1925–57 *Canadian Statistical Review*, 1957 and 1958. 1958–73 Statistics Canada, Census Division.

8. Chile

Calendar year	Cigarettes		Cigars		Tobacco for band-rolled cigarettes and pipe	Total	Population		Consumption per adult	
	Millions	Mn. lbs.	Millions	Mn. lbs.	Mn. lbs.	Mn. lbs.	Total Mns.	15+ Mns.	Cigarettes Number	Total Lbs.
1963	6,438	12·7	2	0·0	0·3	13·0	8·3	5·3*	1,210	2·5
1964	6,576	13·0	2	0·0	0·4	13·3	8·5	5·4*	1,210	2·5
1965	6,810	13·3	2	0·0	0·3	13·7	8·7	5·6*	1,220	2·5
1966	7,008	13·6	2	0·0	0·3	13·9	8·9	5·7*	1,230	2·4
1967	7,038	13·5	1	0·0	0·3	13·8	9·1	5·8*	1,210	2·4
1968	6,841	13·0	1	0·0	0·3	13·2	9·3	6·0*	1,140	2·2
1969	6,853	12·9	1	0·0	0·3	13·2	9·5	6·1*	1,120	2·2
1970	6,752	12·6	1	0·0	0·2	12·9	9·8	6·3*	1,080	2·1
1971	8,233	15·4	1	0·0	0·2	15·7	10·0	6·4*	1,290	2·5
1972	8,334	15·6	1	0·0	0·1	15·8	10·2	6·5*	1,270	2·4
1973	8,835	16·6	1	0·0	0·1	16·7	10·5	6·7*	1,320	2·5

Notes
Details of the numbers and weight of cigarettes and cigars and of the weight of tobacco for hand-rolled cigarettes and pipe were obtained from trade sources.

9. Costa Rica

Calendar year	Cigarettes		Cigarillos		Total Mn. lbs.	Population		Consumption per adult	
	Millions	Mn. lbs.	Millions	Mn. lbs.		Total Mns.	15+ Mns.	Cigarettes Number	Total Lbs.
1963	1,206	2·5	...	...	2·5	1·3	0·6	2,010	4·1
1964	1,255	2·6	...	...	2·6	1·4	0·7	1,790	3·7
1965	1,295	2·6	...	...	2·6	1·4	0·7	1,850	3·8
1966	1,375	2·8	...	...	2·8	1·5	0·7	1,960	3·9
1967	1,394	2·9	0	0·0	2·9	1·5	0·7	1,990	4·1
1968	1,424	2·9	0	0·0	2·9	1·6	0·8	1,780	3·6
1969	1,494	3·1	0	0·0	3·1	1·7	0·8	1,870	3·8
1970	1,568	3·2	0	0·0	3·2	1·7	0·8	1,960	4·0
1971	1,618	2·8	0	0·0	2·8	1·8	0·9	1,800	3·1
1972	1,775	3·0	0	0·0	3·0	1·8	0·9	1,970	3·4
1973	1,858	3·2	0	0·0	3·2	1·9	0·9	2,060	3·5

Notes

(a) Details of the numbers of cigarettes consumed were obtained from trade sources.

(b) Cigarettes were converted from number to weight using a factor of 2·046 lbs. per 1,000 up to 1970. From 1971 onwards the factor used was 1·715 lbs. per 1,000.

(c) Population figures were obtained from *Dirección General de Estadística y Censos*.

21

10. Denmark

Calendar year	Cigarettes Millions	Cigarettes Mn. lbs.	Cigars Millions	Cigars Mn. lbs.	Cigarillos Millions	Cigarillos Mn. lbs.	Smoking tobacco Mn. lbs.	Chewing tobacco Mn. lbs.	Snuff Mn. lbs.	Total Mn. lbs.	Population Total Mns.	Population 15+ Mns.	Consumption per adult Cigarettes Number	Consumption per adult Total Lbs.
1920	860	2·4	321	3·5	86	0·5	5·5	3·1	0·4	15·4	3·2	2·2*	390	7·0
1921	868	2·4	284	3·1	72	0·4	5·2	2·5	0·5	14·1	3·3	2·2	390	6·4
1922	943	2·6	284	3·1	90	0·5	5·1	2·0	0·4	13·7	3·3*	2·3*	410	6·0
1923	1,109	3·1	292	3·2	126	0·7	5·1	2·6	0·6	15·3	3·4*	2·4*	460	6·4
1924	1,159	3·2	285	3·1	125	0·7	4·8	2·5	0·6	14·9	3·4*	2·4*	480	6·2
1925	1,219	3·4	258	2·8	139	0·8	4·7	2·5	0·6	14·8	3·4	2·4*	510	6·2
1926	1,325	3·7	251	2·8	155	0·9	5·1	2·4	0·7	15·6	3·4*	2·4*	550	6·5
1927	1,373	3·8	233	2·6	167	0·9	4·9	2·3	0·7	15·2	3·4*	2·4*	570	6·3
1928	1,544	4·3	222	2·4	196	1·1	5·0	2·2	0·7	15·7	3·5*	2·5*	620	6·3
1929	1,017	2·8	278	3·1	195	1·1	5·0	2·1	0·8	14·9	3·5*	2·5*	410	6·0
1930	1,319	3·6	289	3·2	231	1·3	5·1	2·1	0·8	16·1	3·5	2·6	510	6·2
1931	1,322	3·6	284	3·1	262	1·4	5·0	2·0	0·9	16·0	3·6*	2·6*	510	6·2
1932	1,170	3·2	268	3·0	293	1·6	5·6	1·8	0·9	16·1	3·6	2·6*	450	6·2
1933	1,142	3·2	314	3·5	333	1·8	5·4	1·7	0·9	16·5	3·6	2·7*	420	6·1
1934	1,214	3·4	366	4·0	360	2·0	5·4	1·6	0·9	17·3	3·7	2·7*	450	6·4
1935	1,307	3·6	406	4·5	379	2·1	5·3	1·6	1·0	18·1	3·7	2·8	470	6·5
1936	1,404	3·9	437	4·8	393	2·2	5·6	1·5	1·0	19·0	3·7	2·8*	500	6·8
1937	1,507	4·2	459	5·1	402	2·2	5·3	1·5	1·0	19·3	3·7	2·8	540	6·9
1938	1,605	4·4	469	5·2	407	2·2	5·4	1·4	1·0	19·6	3·8	2·9*	550	6·8
1939	1,748	4·8	487	5·4	425	2·3	5·6	1·3	1·0	20·4	3·8	2·9	600	7·0
1940	1,662	4·6	409	4·5	333	1·8	5·7	1·3	1·1	19·0	3·8	2·9	570	6·6
1941	1,577	4·4	227	2·5	269	1·5	4·4	1·4	1·2	15·4	3·9	2·9*	540	5·3
1942	1,779	4·9	145	1·6	317	1·7	5·7	1·4	1·1	16·4	3·9	3·0*	590	5·5
1943	1,094	3·0	116	1·3	284	1·6	3·8	0·9	1·0	11·6	3·9	3·0*	360	3·9
1944	1,318	3·6	117	1·3	305	1·7	4·1	0·9	1·2	12·8	4·0	3·0*	440	4·3

Denmark (contd)

Calendar year	Cigarettes Millions	Cigarettes Mn. lbs.	Cigars Millions	Cigars Mn. lbs.	Cigarillos Millions	Cigarillos Mn. lbs.	Smoking tobacco Mn. lbs.	Chewing tobacco Mn. lbs.	Snuff Mn. lbs.	Total Mn. lbs.	Population Total Mns.	Population 15+ Mns.	Consumption per adult Cigarettes Number	Consumption per adult Total Lbs.
1945	1,163	3.2	137	1.5	335	1.8	3.1	0.8	1.2	11.6	4.0	3.0	390	3.9
1946	2,150	5.9	308	3.4	474	2.6	5.8	1.2	1.4	20.3	4.1	3.1	690	6.5
1947	2,380	6.6	347	3.8	441	2.4	6.0	1.1	1.2	21.1	4.1	3.1	770	6.8
1948	2,663	7.3	383	4.2	479	2.6	6.8	1.0	1.2	23.1	4.2	3.1	860	7.5
1949	3,489	9.6	383	4.2	402	2.2	5.6	1.0	1.1	23.7	4.2	3.1	1,130	7.6
1950	4,008	11.1	383	4.2	400	2.2	5.5	0.9	1.1	25.0	4.3	3.1	1,290	8.1
1951	3,483	9.6	282	3.1	423	2.3	5.3	0.9	1.1	22.3	4.3	3.2	1,090	7.0
1952	3,881	10.7	214	2.4	542	3.0	5.7	0.8	1.1	23.7	4.3	3.2	1,210	7.4
1953	3,931	10.8	208	2.3	597	3.3	5.7	0.8	1.1	24.0	4.4	3.2	1,230	7.5
1954	3,834	10.6	208	2.3	621	3.4	5.9	0.8	1.1	24.1	4.4	3.2	1,200	7.5
1955	3,787	10.5	216	2.4	612	3.4	5.8	0.7	1.0	23.8	4.4	3.3	1,150	7.2
1956	3,882	10.7	225	2.5	615	3.4	5.7	0.7	1.0	24.0	4.5	3.3	1,180	7.3
1957	4,010	11.1	229	2.5	621	3.4	5.6	0.6	1.0	24.2	4.5	3.3	1,220	7.3
1958	4,349	11.9	239	2.6	657	3.6	5.7	0.6	1.0	25.4	4.5	3.3	1,320	7.7
1959	4,706	13.0	262	2.9	683	3.8	5.4	0.6	1.0	26.7	4.5	3.4	1,380	7.9
1960	4,990	13.6	275	3.0	699	3.8	5.4	0.6	1.0	27.4	4.6	3.4	1,470	8.1
1961	5,097	14.0	286	3.2	705	3.9	5.0	0.5	0.9	27.5	4.6	3.4	1,480	8.1
1962	5,257	14.9	286	3.2	722	4.0	5.0	0.5	0.9	28.5	4.6	3.5	1,500	8.1
1963	5,600	15.0	271	3.0	720	4.0	4.8	0.5	0.9	28.2	4.7	3.5	1,580	8.1
1964	5,277	14.4	293	3.2	854	4.7	5.4	0.5	0.9	29.1	4.7	3.6	1,470	8.1
1965	5,414	15.2	300	3.3	851	4.5	5.4	0.4	0.8	29.6	4.7	3.6	1,500	8.2
1966	5,566	15.6	288	3.2	808	4.4	5.1	0.4	0.8	29.5	4.8	3.6	1,530	8.1
1967	5,614	15.7	290	3.2	809	4.4	5.2	0.4	0.7	29.6	4.8	3.7	1,530	8.1
1968	5,799	16.2	270	3.0	784	4.2	5.1	0.3	0.7	29.5	4.9	3.7	1,570	8.0
1969	6,274	17.5	274	3.0	782	4.2	4.8	0.3	0.6	30.4	4.9	3.7	1,680	8.2
1970	6,357	17.8	267	2.9	762	4.0	4.7	0.3	0.6	30.3	4.9	3.8	1,690	8.1
1971	6,481	18.1	250	2.7	718	3.8	4.6	0.3	0.6	30.1	5.0*	3.8*	1,710	7.9
1972	6,940	19.4	240	2.6	702	3.7	4.3	0.2	0.6	30.8	5.0*	3.8*	1,830	8.1
1973	7,202	20.2	234	2.5	670	3.5	4.2	0.2	0.5	31.1	5.0*	3.9*	1,850	8.0

Notes
(a) Details of the number of cigarettes, cigars and cigarillos and of the weight of pipe tobacco, chewing tobacco and snuff consumed were supplied by Tobaksindustrien, Copenhagen.
(b) Factors for conversion from number to weight for cigarettes, cigars and cigarillos were obtained from trade sources.

11. El Salvador

Calendar year	Cigarettes Millions	Cigarettes Mn. lbs.	Cigars Millions	Cigars Mn. lbs.	Total Mn. lbs.	Population Total Mns.	Population 15+ Mns.	Consumption per adult Cigarettes Number	Consumption per adult Total Lbs.
1964	1,152	2·5	608	3·6	6·1	2·8	1·5	770	4·1
1965	1,202	2·7	541	3·2	5·9	2·9	1·6	750	3·7
1966	1,261	2·8	608	3·6	6·4	3·0	1·6	790	4·0
1967	1,420	3·1	726	4·3	7·4	3·1	1·7	840	4·4
1968	1,541	3·4	557	3·3	6·7	3·2	1·7	910	3·9
1969	1,646	3·6	287	1·7	5·3	3·3	1·8	910	2·9
1970	1,846	4·1	321	1·9	6·0	3·4	1·8	1,030	3·3
1971	1,951	4·3	253	1·5	5·8	3·6	1·9	1,030	3·1
1972	1,989	4·4	287	1·7	6·1	3·7	1·9	1,050	3·2
1973	2,030	4·5	355	2·1	6·6	3·8	2·0	1,020	3·3

Notes

(a) Details of the number of cigarettes and the weight of cigars consumed were obtained from trade sources.

(b) Cigarette consumption in pounds weight has been estimated from the number of cigarettes consumed by using a conversion factor of 2·205 lbs. per 1,000. The conversion factor used for cigars was 5·92 lbs. per 1,000. Cigars figures include local hand-made cigars.

(c) Population figures were taken from *Indicadores Económicos y Sociales del Consejo Nacional de Planificación y Coordinación Económica* (CONAPLAN).

12. Finland

Calendar year	Cigarettes		Cigars		Smoking and chewing tobacco	Snuff	Total	Population		Consumption per adult	
	Millions	Mn. lbs.	Millions	Mn. lbs.	Mn. lbs.	Mn. lbs.	Mn. lbs.	Total Mns.	15+ Mns.	Cigarettes Number	Total Lbs.
1920	2,781	4·2	21	0·2	1·2	0·1	5·7	3·1	2·1	1,320	2·7
1921	2,132	3·2	17	0·2	0·7	0·1	4·2	3·1*	2·1*	1,020	2·0
1922	2,337	3·5	18	0·2	0·7	0·2	4·6	3·2*	2·2*	1,060	2·1
1923	2,835	4·3	25	0·3	1·2	0·2	6·0	3·2*	2·2*	1,290	2·7
1924	3,002	4·5	19	0·2	1·4	0·2	6·3	3·3*	2·3*	1,310	2·7
1925	3,035	4·6	19	0·2	1·1	0·2	6·1	3·3	2·3*	1,320	2·7
1926	3,024	4·5	21	0·2	1·1	0·2	6·0	3·3*	2·3*	1,310	2·6
1927	3,423	5·1	21	0·2	1·0	0·2	6·5	3·3*	2·3*	1,490	2·8
1928	3,616	5·4	21	0·2	1·0	0·2	6·8	3·4*	2·4*	1,510	2·8
1929	3,721	5·6	22	0·2	1·1	0·2	7·1	3·4*	2·4*	1,550	3·0
1930	3,913	5·9	14	0·2	1·1	0·2	7·4	3·4	2·5	1,570	3·0
1931	3,104	4·9	8	0·1	1·0	0·2	6·2	3·5*	2·5*	1,240	2·5
1932	2,960	4·7	9	0·1	1·0	0·1	5·9	3·5	2·5*	1,180	2·4
1933	3,037	5·0	10	0·1	0·9	0·1	6·1	3·5	2·6*	1,170	2·3
1934	3,322	5·8	11	0·1	0·8	0·1	6·8	3·5	2·6*	1,280	2·6
1935	3,497	6·1	12	0·1	0·8	0·1	7·1	3·6	2·6*	1,350	2·7
1936	3,616	6·2	16	0·2	0·9	0·2	7·5	3·6	2·7*	1,340	2·8
1937	3,989	7·1	19	0·2	0·9	0·2	8·4	3·6	2·7	1,480	3·1
1938	4,488	7·7	22	0·2	0·8	0·2	8·9	3·7	2·7*	1,660	3·3
1939	3,963	7·3	19	0·2	1·0	0·2	8·7	3·7	2·7*	1,470	3·2
1940	3,780	6·7	15	0·2	1·0	0·1	8·0	3·7	2·7	1,400	3·0

Finland (contd)

Calendar year	Cigarettes Russian type with hollow mouthpiece		Other types		Total cigarettes		Cigars and cigarillos		Smoking and chewing tobacco	Snuff	Total	Population		Consumption per adult	
	Millions	Mn. lbs.	Millions	Mn. lbs.	Millions	Mn. lbs.	Millions	Mn. lbs.	Mn. lbs.	Mn. lbs.	Mn. lbs.	Total Mns.	15 + Mns.	Cigarettes Number	Total Lbs.
1941	2,080	2·1	2,393	5·9	4,473	8·0	12	0·1	1·0	0·1	9·2	3·7	2·7*	1,660	3·4
1942	2,316	2·3	1,305	3·4	3,621	5·7	7	0·1	0·5	0·1	6·4	3·7	2·7*	1,340	2·4
1943	2,565	2·5	1,059	2·4	3,624	4·9	7	0·1	0·5	0·1	5·6	3·7	2·7*	1,340	2·1
1944	2,414	2·4	511	1·2	2,925	3·6	6	0·1	0·3	0·1	4·1	3·7	2·7*	1,080	1·5
1945	1,866	1·8	274	0·7	2,140	2·5	5	0·1	0·4	0·0	3·0	3·8	2·8	760	1·1
1946	2,094	2·1	792	2·1	2,886	4·2	5	0·1	0·7	0·1	5·1	3·8	2·8	1,030	1·8
1947	2,222	2·2	1,386	3·8	3,608	6·0	6	0·1	1·0	0·1	7·2	3·9	2·8*	1,290	2·6
1948	2,220	2·2	2,038	5·5	4,258	7·7	7	0·1	1·3	0·1	9·2	3·9	2·8	1,520	3·3
1949	1,886	1·9	2,440	6·0	4,326	7·9	9	0·1	1·5	0·1	9·6	4·0	2·8	1,550	3·4
1950	2,104	2·1	2,476	5·9	4,580	8·0	10	0·1	1·8	0·1	10·0	4·0	2·8	1,640	3·6
1951	2,104	2·1	2,562	6·5	4,666	8·6	12	0·1	1·5	0·1	10·3	4·0	2·8	1,670	3·7
1952	2,331	2·3	2,856	7·3	5,187	9·6	13	0·1	1·3	0·1	11·1	4·1	2·8	1,850	4·0
1953	2,320	2·3	2,845	7·1	5,165	9·4	12	0·1	1·1	0·1	10·7	4·1	2·9	1,780	3·7
1954	2,612	2·6	2,949	7·6	5,561	10·2	12	0·1	1·1	0·1	11·5	4·2	2·9	1,920	4·0
1955	2,668	2·6	3,036	7·7	5,704	10·3	13	0·1	0·9	0·1	11·4	4·2	2·9	1,970	3·9
1956	2,653	2·6	3,215	8·1	5,868	10·7	9	0·1	0·8	0·1	11·7	4·3	3·0*	1,960	3·9
1957	2,135	2·1	3,410	8·7	5,545	10·8	9	0·1	1·3	0·1	12·3	4·3	3·0*	1,850	4·1
1958	1,912	1·9	3,329	7·2	5,241	9·1	9	0·1	1·6	0·0	10·8	4·4	3·0	1,775	3·6
1959	1,863	1·8	3,975	8·5	5,838	10·3	10	0·1	1·3	0·0	11·7	4·4	3·0	1,950	3·9
1960	1,723	1·7	4,564	9·3	6,287	11·0	16	0·1	1·1	0·0	12·2	4·4	3·0	2,100	4·1
1961	1,467	1·4	5,154	11·0	6,621	12·4	15	0·1	0·8	0·0	13·3	4·5	3·1	2,140	4·3
1962	1,352	1·3	5,349	11·1	6,701	12·4	18	0·1	1·1	0·0	13·6	4·5	3·1	2,160	4·4
1963	1,393	1·3	5,838	12·8	7,231	14·1	22	0·2*	1·4	0·1	15·8	4·6	3·3	2,190	4·8
1964	950	0·9	4,596	10·1	5,546	11·0	31	0·2*	2·1	0·1	13·4	4·6	3·3	1,680	4·1
1965	920	0·9	5,597	12·3	6,517	13·2	37	0·2*	1·8	0·1	15·3	4·6	3·4	1,920	4·5
1966	750	0·7	5,633	12·4	6,383	13·1	85	0·4*	1·8	0·1	15·4	4·7	3·4	1,880	4·5
1967	629	0·6	6,055	13·3	6,684	13·9	73	0·3	2·1	0·1	16·4	4·7	3·5	1,910	4·7
1968	482	0·5	5,866	12·9	6,348	13·4	72	0·3	2·6	0·1	16·4	4·7	3·5	1,810	4·7
1969	428	0·4	6,107	13·5	6,535	13·9	97	0·4	2·6	0·1	17·0	4·6	3·5	1,870	4·9
1970	350	0·3	6,130	13·5	6,480	13·8	190	0·6	2·2	0·1	16·7	4·6	3·5	1,850	4·8
1971	300	0·3	6,700	14·7	7,000	15·0	140	0·5	2·3	0·0	17·8	4·6	3·5	2,000	5·1
1972	280	0·3	7,300	16·1	7,580	16·4	120	0·5	2·3	0·0	19·2	4·6	3·5	2,170	5·5
1973	240	0·3	7,100	15·6	7,340	15·9	140	0·5	2·2	0·0	18·6	4·7	3·6	2,040	5·2

Notes

(a) Details of the number of cigarettes and cigars and of the weight of pipe and chewing tobacco and snuff consumed were obtained from trade sources.

(b) Factors for conversion from number to weight of cigarettes and cigars were obtained from trade sources.

(c) Details of population growth were obtained from the Central Statistical Office of Finland.

13. France

Calendar year	Cigarettes Millions	Cigarettes Mn. lbs.	Cigars Millions	Cigars Mn. lbs.	Cigarillos Millions	Cigarillos Mn. lbs.	Smoking tobacco Mn. lbs.	Chewing tobacco Mn. lbs.	Snuff Mn. lbs.	Total Mn. lbs.	Population Total Mns.	Population 15+ Mns.	Consumption per adult Cigarettes Number	Consumption per adult Total Lbs.
1932	18,186	48·2	190	1·7	102	0·4	70·8	2·1	5·6	128·8	41·3	31·7*	570	4·1
1933	17,861	47·3	176	1·6	103	0·4	70·6	2·0	5·3	127·2	41·3	31·5*	570	4·0
1934	17,045	45·2	163	1·4	110	0·4	69·8	2·0	5·1	123·9	41·4	31·4*	540	3·9
1935	16,464	43·6	152	1·3	118	0·4	66·6	1·9	4·8	118·6	41·4	31·2	530	3·8
1936	16,952	44·9	157	1·4	130	0·5	67·4	1·9	4·4	120·5	41·3	31·1	550	3·9
1937	17,674	46·8	169	1·5	160	0·6	64·8	1·8	4·1	119·6	41·2	31·3*	560	3·8
1938	18,253	48·4	172	1·5	160	0·6	64·2	1·7	3·8	120·2	41·1	31·4	580	3·8
1939	19,902	52·7	153	1·3	160	0·6	69·8	1·5	3·6	129·5	41·3	31·6*	630	4·1
1940	18,527	49·1	157	1·4	174	0·6	65·8	1·2	3·1	121·2	39·8	30·4	610	4·0
1941	14,924	39·5	67	0·6	114	0·4	53·7	1·3	2·4	97·9	38·8	29·8*	500	3·3
1942	10,918	28·9	60	0·5	114	0·4	32·9	1·1	2·6	66·4	38·7	30·0*	360	2·2
1943	10,001	26·5	58	0·5	81	0·3	25·5	1·0	2·6	56·4	38·5	30·0*	330	1·9
1944	8,878	23·5	41	0·4	85	0·3	20·3	0·7	1·8	47·0	38·3	30·1*	290	1·6
1945	13,233	35·1	46	0·4	87	0·3	31·8	1·0	1·9	70·5	39·1	30·9	430	2·3
1946	18,433	48·8	50	0·4	89	0·3	40·9	1·3	1·9	93·6	40·3	31·5	590	3·0
1947	24,274	64·3	59	0·5	93	0·3	52·7	1·5	2·0	121·3	40·6	31·8	760	3·8
1948	26,089	69·1	53	0·5	78	0·3	58·6	1·6	1·9	132·0	41·0	32·1	810	4·1
1949	27,415	72·6	68	0·6	100	0·4	46·3	1·4	1·7	123·0	41·4	32·4*	850	3·8
1950	30,418	80·6	98	0·9	153	0·5	47·5	1·3	1·7	132·5	41·7	32·7	930	4·1
1951	32,873	87·1	105	0·9	157	0·6	43·6	1·3	1·6	135·1	42·1	32·7*	1,010	4·1
1952	33,824	89·6	102	0·9	189	0·7	40·4	1·3	1·5	134·4	42·4	32·6*	1,040	4·1
1953	36,415	96·5	100	0·9	228	0·8	40·6	1·2	1·4	141·4	42·7	32·6	1,120	4·3
1954	36,801	97·5	105	0·9	239	0·8	39·7	1·2	1·3	141·4	43·0	32·9	1,120	4·3

France (contd)

Calendar year	Cigarettes		Cigars		Cigarillos		Smoking tobacco	Chewing tobacco	Snuff	Total	Population		Consumption per adult	
	Millions	Mn. lbs.	Millions	Mn. lbs.	Millions	Mn. lbs.	Mn. lbs.	Mn. lbs.	Mn. lbs.	Total Mn. lbs.	Total Mns.	15+ Mns.	Cigarettes Number	Total Lbs.
1955	38,315	101·5	118	1·0	275	1·0	38·3	1·2	1·3	144·3	43·3	32·7	1,170	4·4
1956	41,059	108·8	147	1·3	294	1·0	38·5	1·2	1·2	152·0	43·6	33·0	1,240	4·6
1957	42,919	113·7	168	1·5	329	1·2	39·2	1·4	1·1	158·1	44·1	33·2*	1,290	4·8
1958	44,422	117·7	190	1·7	357	1·3	40·3	1·4	1·0	163·4	44·6	33·4*	1,330	4·9
1959	42,284	112·1	214	1·9	323	1·1	39·1	1·3	0·9	156·4	45·1	33·7*	1,250	4·6
1960	44,904	119·0	241	2·1	326	1·2	39·8	1·3	0·9	164·3	45·5	33·9	1,320	4·8
1961	46,638	123·6	264	2·3	351	1·2	40·0	1·2	0·8	169·1	46·0	34·2*	1,360	4·9
1962	48,247	127·9	285	2·5	381	1·3	40·3	1·2	0·8	174·0	46·8	34·7*	1,390	5·0
1963	49,960	132·4	328	2·9	372	1·3	40·6	1·1	0·7	179·0	47·6	35·2	1,420	5·1
1964	50,767	134·5	378	3·3	371	1·3	38·1	1·2	0·7	179·1	48·4	36·0	1,410	5·0
1965	54,533	144·5	406	3·6	393	1·4	36·7	1·1	0·7	188·0	48·8*	36·2*	1,510	5·2
1966	57,053	151·2	440	3·9	416	1·5	35·2	1·1	0·6	193·5	49·2*	36·6*	1,560	5·3
1967	60,377	160·0	451	4·0	434	1·5	34·2	1·1	0·6	201·4	49·6	37·1	1,630	5·4
1968	63,282	167·7	491	4·3	425	1·5	34·3	1·1	0·5	209·4	50·0	37·6	1,680	5·6
1969	65,844	174·5	532	4·7	410	1·4	31·6	1·1	0·5	213·8	50·1	37·5	1,760	5·7
1970	69,650	184·6	546	4·8	426	1·5	29·4	1·1	0·4	221·8	50·5	38·0	1,830	5·8
1971	72,143	191·1	656	5·8	411	1·4	27·6	1·1	0·4	227·4	51·0	38·3	1,880	5·9
1972	72,070	191·0	710	6·3	398	1·4	25·4	1·1	0·3	225·5	51·5	38·8	1,860	5·8
1973	75,379	197·7	795	7·0	378	1·3	23·6	1·1	0·3	233·0	51·9	39·2	1,920	5·9

Notes

Details of the quantities of tobacco products consumed and factors for conversion from number to weight were provided by the French Tobacco Monopoly. These factors were as follows: cigarettes 2·650 lbs. per 1,000, cigars 8·820 lbs. per 1,000 and cigarillos 3·528 lbs. per 1,000.

14. Germany (1926-39) and Western Germany (1949-73)

Year ended 31st March	Cigarettes		Cigars		Fine-cut tobacco	Pipe tobacco	Total	Population		Consumption per adult	
	Millions	Mn. lbs.	Millions	Mn. lbs.	Mn. lbs.	Mn. lbs.	Mn. lbs.	Total Mns.	15+ Mns.	Cigarettes Number	Total Lbs.
1926	30,529	67·3	5,746	67·2		71·9	206·4	63·2	47·1	650	4·4
1927	29,156	64·3	5,980	70·0		84·9	219·2	63·6	47·4*	620	4·6
1928	32,768	72·3	6,635	77·6		84·9	234·8	64·0	47·8*	690	4·9
1929	31,601	69·7	6,589	77·1		82·9	229·7	64·4	48·2*	660	4·8
1930	32,877	72·5	6,973	81·6		82·4	236·5	64·7	48·4*	680	4·9
1931	29,367	64·8	7,146	83·6		86·3	234·7	65·1	48·8*	600	4·8
1932	28,064	61·9	6,194	72·5		70·8	205·2	65·4	49·1*	570	4·2
1933	31,759	70·0	5,678	66·4	33·9	41·0	211·3	65·7	49·3*	640	4·3
1934	33,701	74·3	6,570	76·9	30·6	42·3	224·1	66·0	49·6	680	4·5
1935	36,162	79·7	7,854	91·9	29·5	40·8	241·9	66·4	50·1*	720	4·8
1936	37,471	82·6	7,892	92·3	31·3	38·3	244·5	66·9	50·6*	740	4·8
1937	38,455	84·8	8,424	98·6	33·4	36·5	253·3	67·3	51·1*	750	5·0
1938	42,420	93·5	8,932	104·5	36·1	33·5	267·6	67·8	51·7*	820	5·2
1939	47,306	104·3	9,150	107·1	40·1	30·4	281·9	68·9	52·7*	900	5·3
1949	9,852	21·7	1,453	18·3	15·2	4·4	59·6	48·3	36·9*	270	1·6
Calendar Year											
1950	24,089	58·4	3,785	50·1	38·2	10·7	157·4	50·0	38·4	630	4·1
1951	28,967	70·2	4,157	55·9	38·2	10·8	175·1	50·5	38·8	750	4·5
1952	30,840	74·8	4,592	61·5	35·1	9·9	181·3	50·8	39·3*	780	4·6
1953	35,868	86·9	4,520	60·8	31·6	8·6	187·9	51·4	39·9*	900	4·7
1954	39,663	96·2	4,472	60·5	29·2	7·6	193·5	51·9	40·6	980	4·8
1955	45,411	110·1	4,585	61·6	26·9	7·2	205·8	52·4	41·2	1,100	5·0
1956	50,663	122·9	4,601	61·9	23·5	6·5	214·8	53·0	42·0	1,210	5·1
1957	55,875	138·1	4,724	57·8	21·3	5·8	223·0	53·6	42·4	1,320	5·3
1958	60,482	149·5	4,629	56·7	19·3	5·3	203·8	54·3	42·9	1,410	5·4
1959	65,245	155·3	4,544	55·6	19·7	5·0	235·6	54·9	43·4	1,500	5·4

Germany (1926–39) and Western Germany (1949–73) (contd)

Calendar year	Cigarettes		Cigars		Fine-cut tobacco	Pipe tobacco	Total	Population		Consumption per adult	
	Millions	Mn. lbs.	Millions	Mn. lbs.	Mn. lbs.	Mn. lbs.	Mn. lbs.	Total Mns.	15 + Mns.	Cigarettes Number	Total Lbs.
1960	70,956	168·9	4,349	53·2	18·3	4·4	244·8	55·4	43·6	1,630	5·6
1961	78,039	178·6	4,111	60·4	17·4	4·0	260·4	56·2	44·0	1,770	5·9
1962	83,286	188·6	3,988	56·9	16·6	3·6	265·7	56·9	44·4	1,880	6·0
1963	85,276	190·6	3,786	51·9	16·7	3·4	262·6	57·6	44·8	1,900	5·9
1964	90,156	200·1	4,098	53·3	17·3	3·9	274·6	58·3	45·2	1,990	6·1
1965	96,055	212·1	3,953	51·8	15·6	3·3	282·8	59·0	45·7	2,100	6·2
1966	101,488	225·9	3,778	51·5	15·0	3·3	295·7	59·6	46·0*	2,210	6·4
1967	99,139	213·8	3,597	52·0	15·3	4·5	285·6	59·9	46·1	2,150	6·2
1968	105,444	231·9	3,595	48·8	14·3	4·4	299·4	60·2	46·3	2,280	6·5
1969	112,431	243·6	3,420	46·8	13·2	4·2	307·8	60·8	46·7	2,410	6·6
1970	118,051	255·8	3,212	43·9	12·8	4·3	316·8	60·7	47·0	2,510	6·7
1971	125,493	271·9	3,100	42·4	10·9	4·0	329·2	61·3	47·2	2,660	7·0
1972	126,469	274·0	3,051	41·7	11·7	4·6	332·0	61·7	47·7	2,650	7·0
1973	125,461	271·8	2,802	38·1	13·1	4·5	327·5	62·1	48·0	2,610	6·8

Notes
(a) Details of the number of cigarettes and cigars and of the weight of fine-cut, pipe and other manufactured tobacco consumed were obtained from the following sources:
1926–49 *Bevölkerung und Wirtschaft*, 1871–1957, published by the Western Germany Federal Statistics Office, Wiesbaden.
1930–63 Estimates from trade sources converted to a calendar year basis.
1964–73 *Finanzen und Steuern – Absatz von Tabakwaren*, published by the Western Germany Federal Statistics Office, Wiesbaden.
(b) Cigarette consumption in pounds weight was estimated from the number of cigarettes consumed by using a conversion factor of 2·205 lbs. per 1,000 up until 1949. From 1950 onwards the conversion factors were provided from trade sources. The conversion factors for cigars were obtained from trade sources for the whole period.
(c) The figures for 1949 onwards include cigarettes which were produced in West Berlin and represent the consumption of tobacco goods in Western Germany including West Berlin.
(d) The sources of the population figures were as follows:
1926–39 *Bevölkerung und Wirtschaft*, 1871–1957, published by the Western Germany Federal Statistics Office, Wiesbaden.
1949–63 United Nations Demographic Yearbook.
1964–73 *Statistiches Jahrbuch für die Bundesrepublik Deutschland*, published by the Western Germany Federal Statistics Office, Wiesbaden.

15. Ghana

Calendar year	Cigarettes		Cigars and cigarillos		Tobacco for hand-rolled cigarettes, pipe and snuff	Total	Population		Consumption per adult	
	Millions	Mn. lbs.	Millions	Mn. lbs.	Mn. lbs.	Mn. lbs.	Total Mns.	15 + Mns.	Cigarettes Number	Total Lbs.
1964	1,729	3·8	0	0·0	0·4	4·2	7·4	4·2	410	1·0
1965	2,078	4·6	0	0·0	0·3	4·9	7·6	4·3	480	1·1
1966	1,869	4·1	0	0·0	0·3	4·4	7·8	4·4	420	1·0
1967	1,779	3·9	0	0·0	0·4	4·3	7·9	4·5	400	1·0
1968	1,869	4·1	0	0·0	0·7	4·8	8·2	4·7	400	1·0
1969	1,901	4·2	0	0·0	0·8	5·0	8·4	4·8	400	1·0
1970	1,997	4·4	0	0·0	1·0	5·4	8·6	4·6	430	1·2
1971	2,031	4·5	0	0·0	0·9	5·4	8·9	4·7	430	1·2
1972	1,986	4·4	0	0·0	0·9	5·3	9·1	4·8	410	1·1
1973	2,356	5·2	0	0·0	1·0	6·2	9·3	4·9	480	1·3

Notes
(a) Details of tobacco consumed by products were obtained from Central Bureau of Statistics and from trade sources.
(b) Cigarette consumption in pounds weight has been estimated from the number of cigarettes consumed by using a conversion factor of 2·205 lbs. per 1,000.
(c) Population figures were obtained from Census Office.

16. Greece

Calendar year	Cigarettes Millions	Mn. lbs.	Total Mn. lbs.	Population Total Mns.	15+ Mns.	Consumption per adult Cigarettes Number	Total Lbs.
1920	3,937	9·9	9·9	5·0	3·3	1,190	3·0
1921	5,203	13·0	13·0	5·0	3·3*	1,580	3·9
1922	5,439	13·6	13·6	5·2*	3·4*	1,600	4·0
1923	4,725	11·8	11·8	5·5*	3·7*	1,280	3·2
1924	4,663	11·7	11·7	5·8*	3·9*	1,200	3·0
1925	5,323	13·3	13·3	6·0	4·0*	1,330	3·3
1926	4,310	10·8	10·8	6·0*	4·0*	1,080	2·7
1927	4,221	10·6	10·6	6·1*	4·1*	1,030	2·6
1928	4,115	10·3	10·3	6·2	4·2	980	2·5
1929	4,234	10·6	10·6	6·3*	4·3*	980	2·5
1930	4,123	10·3	10·3	6·4	4·3*	960	2·4
1931	4,048	10·1	10·1	6·4*	4·3*	940	2·3
1932	3,796	9·5	9·5	6·5	4·4*	860	2·2
1933	4,049	10·1	10·1	6·6	4·5*	900	2·2
1934	4,256	10·7	10·7	6·7	4·5*	950	2·4
1935	4,434	11·1	11·1	6·8	4·6*	960	2·4
1936	4,625	11·6	11·6	6·9	4·6*	1,010	2·5
1937	4,655	11·7	11·7	7·0	4·7*	990	2·5
1938	5,076	12·7	12·7	7·1	4·7*	1,080	2·7
1939	5,179	13·0	13·0	7·2	4·8*	1,080	2·7
1940	5,490	13·8	13·8	7·3	4·9	1,120	2·8
1941	4,734	11·9	11·9	7·4	5·0*	950	2·4
1942	4,964	12·4	12·4	7·3	5·0*	990	2·5
1943	4,197	10·5	10·5	7·3	5·0*	840	2·1
1944	2,345	5·9	5·9	7·3	5·0*	470	1·2
1945	4,248	10·6	10·6	7·3	5·0*	850	2·1
1946	6,136	15·4	15·4	7·4	5·1*	1,200	3·0
1947	7,447	18·7	18·7	7·5	5·2*	1,430	3·6
1948	7,841	19·6	19·6	7·7	5·4*	1,450	3·6
1949	8,447	21·2	21·2	7·5	5·3	1,590	4·0

Greece (contd)

Calendar year	Cigarettes			Population		Consumption per adult	
	Millions	Total Mn. lbs.	Mn. lbs.	Total Mns.	15+ Mns.	Cigarettes Number	Total Lbs.
1950	8,656	21·7	21·7	7·6	5·4*	1,600	4·0
1951	8,607	21·6	21·6	7·6	5·5	1,560	3·9
1952	8,595	21·5	21·5	7·7	5·6*	1,530	3·8
1953	8,871	22·2	22·2	7·8	5·7	1,560	3·9
1954	8,964	22·5	22·5	7·9	5·8*	1,550	3·9
1955	9,187	23·0	23·0	8·0	5·9	1,560	3·9
1956	9,206	23·1	23·1	8·0	6·0*	1,530	3·9
1957	9,578	24·0	24·0	8·1	6·0*	1,600	4·0
1958	10,074	25·2	25·2	8·1	6·0	1,680	4·2
1959	10,335	25·9	25·9	8·1	6·0	1,720	4·3
1960	10,563	26·5	26·5	8·2	6·1	1,730	4·3
1961	10,820	27·1	27·1	8·3	6·1	1,770	4·4
1962	11,135	27·9	27·9	8·4	6·2	1,800	4·5
1963	11,719	29·3	29·3	8·4	6·3	1,860	4·7
1964	11,894	29·8	29·8	8·5	6·3	1,890	4·7
1965	12,328	31·1	31·1	8·5	6·4	1,930	4·9
1966	13,073	32·7	32·7	8·6	6·5	2,010	5·0
1967	13,644	34·1	34·1	8·7	6·5	2,100	5·2
1968	14,066	35·2	35·2	8·8	6·6	2,130	5·3
1969	14,432	36·1	36·1	8·8	6·6	2,190	5·4
1970	15,144	37·9	37·9	8·9	6·7	2,260	5·7
1971	15,300	38·2	38·2	8·9	6·7	2,290	5·7
1972	16,250	40·3	40·3	9·0	6·7	2,410	6·0
1973	17,360	43·1	43·1	9·1	6·8	2,550	6·3

Notes

Details of the weight of cigarettes consumed and the factor for conversion from weight to numbers were provided by the National Tobacco Board of Greece. Consumption of other manufactured tobacco goods in Greece is negligible.

17. Hong Kong

Calendar year	Cigarettes		Cigars		European smoking tobacco	Chinese prepared tobacco†	Total	Population		Consumption per adult	
	Millions	Mn. lbs.	Millions	Mn. lbs.	Mn. lbs.	Mn. lbs.	Mn. lbs.	Total Mns.	15 + Mns.	Cigarettes Number	Total Lbs.
1964	6,373	12·8	...	0·1	0·1	0·5	13·5	3·4	2·0	3,230	6·8
1965	6,737	13·5	...	0·1	0·1	0·5	14·1	3·5	2·0	3,310	6·9
1966	6,734	13·6	...	0·1	0·1	0·5	14·1	3·6	2·1	3,210	6·7
1967	5,967	12·0	...	0·1	0·1	0·4	12·5	3·6	2·1	2,780	5·8
1968	6,582	13·2	...	0·1	0·1	0·4	13·8	3·7	2·2	2,940	6·2
1969	6,289	12·6	...	0·1	0·1	0·4	13·2	3·8	2·3	2,720	5·7
1970	6,429	12·8	...	0·1	0·1	0·3	13·3	3·9	2·4	2,670	5·5
1971	6,804	13·4	...	0·1	0·1	0·3	13·9	4·0	2·5	2,720	5·5
1972	7,119	14·0	...	0·1	0·1	0·3	14·5	4·0	2·6	2,750	5·6
1973	7,459	14·4	...	0·1	0·1	0·3	14·9	4·1	2·7	2,780	5·5

† Used for hand-rolled cigarettes.

Notes

(a) Details of the weight of cigarettes, cigars, European smoking tobaccos and Chinese prepared tobaccos were obtained from Commerce and Industry Department, Hong Kong Government.

(b) Factors for conversion from weight to count for cigarettes were obtained from Commerce and Industry Department, Hong Kong Government and trade sources. A conversion factor for cigars was not available because of the large variations of weight amongst cigar products.

(c) Population figures were projected by referring to the best estimates and census results compiled by Census and Statistics Department, Hong Kong Government.

18. Iceland

Calendar year	Cigarettes		Cigars		Smoking tobacco	Snuff	Total†	Population		Consumption per adult	
	Millions	Mn. lbs.	Millions	Mn. lbs.	Mn. lbs.	Mn. lbs.	Mn. lbs.	Total Mns.	15+ Mns.	Cigarettes Number	Total Lbs.
1932	37	0·08	0	0·01	0·04	0·08	0·23	0·11	0·08*	470	3·0
1933	48	0·11	1	0·01	0·04	0·08	0·25	0·11	0·08*	610	3·2
1934	55	0·12	1	0·01	0·04	0·06	0·26	0·11	0·08*	690	3·3
1935	39	0·09	1	0·01	0·03	0·07	0·22	0·12	0·08*	480	2·7
1936	32	0·07	1	0·01	0·04	0·07	0·20	0·12	0·08*	400	2·5
1937	36	0·08	1	0·01	0·04	0·07	0·22	0·12	0·08*	440	2·6
1938	38	0·08	1	0·01	0·04	0·10	0·26	0·12	0·08*	460	3·1
1939	27	0·06	1	0·01	0·04	0·07	0·19	0·12	0·08*	320	2·3
1940	54	0·12	1	0·01	0·07	0·04	0·25	0·12	0·09	640	2·9
1941	66	0·15	1	0·02	0·05	0·06	0·28	0·12	0·09*	770	3·3
1942	76	0·17	2	0·02	0·04	0·07	0·31	0·12	0·09*	880	3·6
1943	72	0·16	3	0·05	0·01	0·08	0·30	0·13	0·09*	820	3·4
1944	77	0·17	2	0·02	0·02	0·08	0·29	0·13	0·09*	870	3·3
1945	112	0·25	1	0·01	0·03	0·07	0·37	0·13	0·09*	1,230	4·1
1946	167	0·37	3	0·04	0·04	0·07	0·53	0·13	0·09*	1,800	5·7
1947	157	0·35	2	0·02	0·03	0·10	0·50	0·13	0·09	1,670	5·3
1948	159	0·35	1	0·01	0·05	0·08	0·49	0·14	0·10*	1,670	5·2
1949	143	0·32	2	0·02	0·03	0·08	0·46	0·14	0·10	1,470	4·7
1950	148	0·33	2	0·02	0·05	0·08	0·48	0·14	0·10	1,490	4·9
1951	141	0·31	1	0·01	0·03	0·08	0·43	0·15	0·10*	1,410	4·3
1952	138	0·31	1	0·01	0·05	0·08	0·44	0·15	0·10*	1,370	4·4
1953	162	0·36	2	0·02	0·05	0·08	0·51	0·15	0·10*	1,590	5·0
1954	145	0·32	2	0·03	0·04	0·08	0·47	0·15	0·10*	1,410	4·6

† In addition to the goods listed above, the total column includes a small amount of chewing tobacco which was consumed in early years in Iceland.

Iceland (contd)

Calendar year	Cigarettes		Cigars		Smoking tobacco	Snuff	Total	Population		Consumption per adult	
	Millions	Mn. lbs.	Millions	Mn. lbs.	Mn. lbs.	Mn. lbs.	Total Mn. lbs.	Total Mns.	15+ Mns.	Cigarettes Number	Total Lbs.
1955	151	0·33	2	0·03	0·04	0·08	0·48	0·16	0·11*	1,420	4·6
1956	173	0·38	2	0·02	0·04	0·08	0·52	0·16	0·11*	1,620	4·9
1957	199	0·44	2	0·03	0·05	0·09	0·60	0·16	0·11*	1,840	5·6
1958	197	0·43	4	0·05	0·04	0·07	0·60	0·17	0·11*	1,790	5·5
1959	194	0·43	4	0·06	0·04	0·08	0·60	0·17	0·11*	1,730	5·4
1960	196	0·43	4	0·05	0·05	0·07	0·61	0·18	0·11	1,720	5·3
1961	217	0·48	4	0·06	0·06	0·07	0·67	0·18	0·12*	1,850	5·8
1962	229	0·50	5	0·08	0·07	0·07	0·72	0·18	0·12*	1,920	6·1
1963	243	0·54	7	0·10	0·06	0·07	0·77	0·19	0·12*	2,010	6·4
1964	202	0·45	9	0·14	0·10	0·07	0·76	0·19	0·12*	1,640	6·2
1965	232	0·51	10	0·15	0·09	0·07	0·82	0·19	0·13*	1,840	6·5
1966	258	0·57	11	0·17	0·09	0·07	0·90	0·20	0·13*	2,000	7·0
1967	270	0·60	12	0·18	0·09	0·07	0·94	0·20	0·13*	2,080	7·2
1968	250	0·55	10	0·15	0·13	0·07	0·91	0·20	0·13*	1,880	6·8
1969	221	0·49	10	0·15	0·20	0·06	0·90	0·20	0·14*	1,630	6·6
1970	254	0·56	11	0·17	0·18	0·06	0·97	0·20	0·14	1,830	7·0
1971	253	0·56	13	0·20	0·15	0·06	0·96	0·21	0·14*	1,780	6·8
1972	291	0·64	16	0·24	0·14	0·06	1·08	0·21	0·14*	2,020	7·5
1973	298	0·66	18	0·27	0·13	0·05	1·10	0·21	0·15*	2,030	7·5

Notes

(a) Details of the weight of tobacco consumed by types of product were provided by the State Wine, Spirit and Tobacco Authority, Reykjavik.

(b) The numbers of cigarettes consumed have been estimated from the cigarette consumption in pounds weight by using a conversion factor of 2·205 lbs. per 1,000. The conversion factor used for cigars was 15 lbs. per 1,000.

19. India

Calendar year	Cigarettes		Cigars and cheroots		Biris		Snuff	Hookah tobacco	Chewing tobacco	Total†	Population		Consumption per adult	
	Millions	Mn. lbs.	Millions	Mn. lbs.	Millions	Mn. lbs.	Mn. lbs.	Mn. lbs.	Mn. lbs.	Mn. lbs.	Total Mns.	15+ Mns.	Cigarettes Number	Total Lbs.
1948	17,191	43·6	4,609	50·7	89,200	89·2	4·4	103·8	124·6	416·6	349·4	217·7	80	1·9
1949	22,095	56·1	4,518	49·7	90,900	90·9	5·3	110·2	127·5	440·0	353·8	220·8	100	2·0
1950	21,606	54·8	4,673	51·4	101,600	101·6	5·6	118·5	128·9	461·1	358·3	223·9	100	2·1
1951	21,048	53·4	4,136	45·5	113,900	113·9	7·9	120·6	116·9	458·5	362·8	227·1	90	2·0
1952	18,527	47·0	3,736	41·1	120,200	120·2	7·9	128·0	109·7	454·2	369·7	230·3	80	2·0
1953	19,768	50·2	3,526	38·8	118,600	118·6	8·4	124·2	109·1	449·6	376·8	233·5	80	1·9
1954	21,252	53·9	3,816	42·0	121,600	121·6	9·4	120·5	114·8	462·5	383·9	236·8	90	2·0
1955	22,829	57·9	4,109	45·2	145,500	145·5	9·7	123·7	118·2	500·5	391·2	240·1	100	2·1
1956	26,303	66·7	4,036	44·4	130,700	130·7	9·9	118·2	121·4	491·6	398·6	243·5	110	2·0
1957	28,892	73·3	3,927	43·2	141,100	141·1	9·1	103·0	117·5	487·5	406·2	246·9	120	2·0
1958	29,840	75·7	4,182	46·0	150,500	150·5	10·0	95·0	127·1	504·6	413·9	250·3	120	2·0
1959	32,166	81·6	4,164	45·8	149,200	149·2	11·3	96·0	129·6	513·8	421·2	253·8	130	2·0
1960	38,334	97·3	4,073	44·8	156,500	156·5	12·2	94·9	133·2	539·2	429·7	257·4	150	2·1
1961	39,470	100·0	4,136	45·5	171,600	171·6	12·8	95·6	137·2	563·0	439·2	263·1	150	2·1
1962	40,000	101·5	3,845	42·3	149,200	149·2	12·3	91·8	141·0	538·4	448·9	268·9	150	2·0
1963	39,593	100·4	3,500	38·5	136,099	136·1	9·5	71·7	119·4	475·9	458·8	274·8	140	1·7
1964	45,217	114·7	3,391	37·3	146,812	146·8	10·2	70·0	118·5	497·8	468·9	280·8	160	1·8
1965	51,853	131·6	3,377	37·1	149,804	149·8	9·5	69·8	118·2	516·3	479·2	287·0	180	1·8
1966	54,929	139·4	3,304	36·3	153,572	153·6	8·6	65·2	117·4	520·8	489·7	293·3	190	1·8
1967	54,310	137·8	3,295	36·2	154,584	154·6	9·9	69·3	117·3	525·4	500·5	299·8	180	1·8
1968	58,230	147·7	3,360	37·0	156,255	156·3	10·0	62·0	116·8	530·1	511·5	306·4	190	1·7
1969	60,181	152·7	3,125	34·4	165,935	165·9	9·9	60·6	113·6	537·4	522·8	313·1	190	1·7
1970	61,784	156·7	3,010	33·1	171,930	171·9	9·9	58·5	112·1	542·5	534·3	320·0	190	1·7
1971	61,141	155·1	2,988	32·9	173,118	173·1	9·8	62·1	111·8	545·2	547·9	328·8	190	1·7
1972	57,549	146·0	2,550	28·1	170,124	170·1	10·5	52·0	102·5	509·7	560·0	336·0	170	1·5
1973	58,375	148·1	2,405	26·5	171,579	171·6	9·5	46·1	95·5	497·6	572·3	343·4	170	1·4

† In addition to the goods listed, the total column includes at least 300,000 lbs. weight of smoking tobaccos which is consumed annually in India.

Notes

(a) Details of the numbers of cigarettes cleared for home consumption were provided by the Indian Council of Agricultural Research, New Delhi, for the years 1955 to 1960 were published by the Government of India's Central Statistical Organisation.

(b) Consumption figures in pounds weight for the years 1961 to 1973 for cigarettes, cigars and cheroots, biris, snuff, hookah tobacco and chewing tobacco were supplied to The Regional Office (Tobacco) Indian Council of Agricultural Research by the Central Board of Revenue (Excise and Customs), New Delhi, and have been adjusted from a fiscal year to a calendar year basis.

(c) Cigarette consumption in pounds weight has been estimated from the number of cigarettes consumed by using a conversion factor of 2·537 lbs. per 1,000. The conversion factors used for cigars and for biris were 11 lbs. per 1,000 and 1 lb. per 1,000 respectively.

20. Indonesia

Year ended 30th September	Cigarettes		Kreteks†		Total Mn. lbs.	Population		Consumption per adult	
	Millions	Mn. lbs.	Millions	Mn. lbs.		Total Mns.	15+ Mns.	Cigarettes Number‡	Total Lbs.
1969	14,800	32·6	24,000	95·2	127·8	114·9	70·4*	210	1·8
1970	13,963	30·8	18,684	74·1	104·9	117·5	71·9*	190	1·5
1971	14,847	32·7	22,236	88·2	120·9	120·1	73·5*	200	1·6
1972	15,907	35·1	22,560	89·5	124·6	123·1	75·3*	210	1·7
1973	17,598	38·8	25,399	100·8	139·6	126·1	77·2*	230	1·8
1974	24,906	54·9	29,012	115·1	170·0	129·1	79·0*	320	2·2

† A kretek is a cigarette which contains a significant portion of non-tobacco material, traditionally cloves.

‡ Excludes kreteks.

Notes

(a) Details of the numbers of cigarettes and kreteks consumed were obtained from the Directorate General of Customs and Excise and from the Directorate General of Light Industries.

(b) Cigarette consumption in pounds weight was estimated from the number of cigarettes consumed by using a conversion factor of 2·205 lbs. per 1,000. The conversion factor used for kreteks was 3·968 lbs. per 1,000.

(c) Population figures were obtained from the Central Bureau of Statistics, Jakarta.

21. The Republic of Ireland

Calendar year	Cigarettes		Cigars		Smoking tobacco	Snuff	Total	Population		Consumption per adult	
	Millions	Mn. lbs.	Millions	Mn. lbs.	Mn. lbs.	Mn. lbs.	Total Mn. lbs.	Total Mns.	15+ Mns.	Cigarettes Number	Total Lbs.
1920	1,406	3·1	0	0·0	5·5	0·3	8·9	3·1	2·2*	640	4·0
1921	1,361	3·0	0	0·0	5·5	0·3	8·8	3·1*	2·2*	620	4·0
1922	1,315	2·9	0	0·0	5·3	0·3	8·5	3·1*	2·2*	600	3·9
1923	1,361	3·0	0	0·0	4·9	0·3	8·2	3·0*	2·1*	650	3·9
1924	1,406	3·1	0	0·0	4·9	0·3	8·3	3·0*	2·1*	670	4·0
1925	1,497	3·3	0	0·0	4·9	0·3	8·5	3·0	2·1*	710	4·0
1926	1,542	3·4	0	0·0	4·7	0·3	8·4	3·0	2·1	730	4·0
1927	1,633	3·6	0	0·0	4·6	0·3	8·5	3·0*	2·1*	780	4·0
1928	1,723	3·8	0	0·0	4·5	0·3	8·6	3·0*	2·1*	820	4·1
1929	1,814	4·0	0	0·0	4·4	0·3	8·7	2·9*	2·1*	860	4·1
1930	1,950	4·3	0	0·0	4·4	0·3	9·0	2·9	2·1*	930	4·3
1931	2,132	4·7	0	0·0	4·2	0·3	9·2	2·9*	2·1*	1,020	4·4
1932	2,222	4·9	0	0·0	3·8	0·3	9·0	2·9	2·1*	1,060	4·3
1933	2,313	5·1	0	0·0	3·8	0·2	9·1	3·0	2·1*	1,100	4·3
1934	2,494	5·5	0	0·0	3·6	0·2	9·3	3·0	2·1*	1,190	4·4
1935	2,540	5·6	0	0·0	3·6	0·2	9·4	3·0	2·1*	1,210	4·5
1936	2,585	5·7	0	0·0	3·6	0·2	9·5	3·0	2·1	1,230	4·5
1937	2,721	6·0	0	0·0	3·6	0·2	9·8	2·9	2·1*	1,300	4·7
1938	2,900	6·4	0	0·0	3·5	0·2	10·1	2·9	2·1*	1,380	4·8
1939	3,038	6·7	0	0·0	3·3	0·2	10·2	2·9	2·1*	1,450	4·9
1940	3,175	7·0	0	0·0	3·1	0·2	10·3	3·0	2·2*	1,440	4·7
1941	2,766	6·1	0	0·0	2·8	0·2	9·1	3·0	2·2	1,260	4·1
1942	2,766	6·1	0	0·0	2·8	0·2	9·1	3·0	2·2*	1,260	4·1
1943	3,175	7·0	0	0·0	3·0	0·2	10·2	2·9	2·1*	1,510	4·9
1944	3,401	7·5	0	0·0	3·1	0·2	10·8	2·9	2·1*	1,620	5·1
1945	3,265	7·2	0	0·0	3·2	0·2	10·6	3·0	2·1*	1,550	5·0
1946	4,127	9·1	0	0·0	3·3	0·2	12·6	3·0	2·1	1,970	6·0
1947	4,354	9·6	0	0·0	3·0	0·2	12·8	3·0	2·1*	2,070	6·1
1948	4,580	10·1	0	0·0	2·7	0·2	13·0	3·0	2·1*	2,180	6·2
1949	4,989	11·0	0	0·0	2·8	0·2	14·0	3·0	2·1*	2,380	6·7

The Republic of Ireland (contd)

Calendar year	Cigarettes Millions	Cigarettes Mn. lbs.	Cigars Millions	Cigars Mn. lbs.	Smoking tobacco Mn. lbs.	Snuff Mn. lbs.	Total Mn. lbs.	Population Total Mns.	Population 15+ Mns.	Consumption per adult Cigarettes Number	Consumption per adult Total Lbs.
1950	5,261	11·6	0	0·0	2·8	0·1	14·5	3·0	2·1*	2,510	6·9
1951	5,941	13·1	0	0·0	2·7	0·1	15·9	3·0	2·1	2,830	7·6
1952	5,578	12·3	0	0·0	2·1	0·1	14·5	2·9	2·1*	2,660	6·9
1953	5,400	11·8	0	0·0	2·5	0·1	14·4	2·9	2·1*	2,570	6·9
1954	5,220	11·5	0	0·0	2·1	0·1	13·7	2·9	2·1*	2,490	6·5
1955	5,500	12·1	0	0·0	2·2	0·1	14·4	2·9	2·1*	2,620	6·9
1956	5,027	11·1	0	0·0	1·9	0·1	13·1	2·9	2·0	2,510	6·6
1957	4,850	10·8	0	0·0	1·8	0·1	12·7	2·9	2·0*	2,430	6·4
1958	4,765	10·6	0	0·0	1·8	0·1	12·5	2·9	2·0*	2,380	6·3
1959	4,942	10·9	0	0·0	1·7	0·1	12·7	2·8	2·0*	2,470	6·4
1960	5,115	11·3	0	0·0	1·6	0·1	13·0	2·8	2·0*	2,560	6·5
1961	5,325	11·7	0	0·0	1·6	0·1	13·4	2·8	1·9	2,800	7·1
1962	5,270	11·5	0	0·0	1·6	0·1	13·2	2·8	1·9*	2,770	6·9
1963	5,570	12·1	0	0·0	1·6	0·1	13·8	2·8	2·0*	2,780	6·9
1964	5,360	11·6	12	0·1	1·7	0·0	13·4	2·8	2·0*	2,680	6·7
1965	5,380	11·5	12	0·1	1·6	0·0	13·2	2·9	2·0*	2,690	6·6
1966	5,530	11·7	12	0·1	1·4	0·0	13·2	2·9	2·0	2,790	6·7
1967	5,603	11·6	16	0·1	1·4	0·0	13·1	2·9	2·0	2,820	6·6
1968	5,700	11·6	16	0·1	1·3	0·0	13·0	2·9	2·0	2,850	6·5
1969	5,925	11·7	23	0·1	1·3	0·0	13·1	2·9	2·0	2,950	6·5
1970	6,070	11·6	30	0·1	1·2	0·0	12·9	2·9	2·0	2,990	6·4
1971	6,105	11·6	40	0·2	1·3	0·0	13·1	3·0	2·1	2,980	6·4
1972	6,510	12·2	55	0·2	1·2	0·0	13·6	3·0	2·1*	3,140	6·6
1973	6,975	12·9	55	0·2	1·2	0·0	14·3	3·0	2·1*	3,340	6·8
1974	7,500	13·6	60	0·2	1·2	0·0	15·0	3·0	2·1*	3,550	7·1

Notes

Details of the weight of cigarettes, smoking tobacco and snuff consumed for the years 1954–56 were obtained from the *Irish Trade Journal and Statistical Bulletin* and the *Trade Statistics of Ireland*. For the years 1920–53 and 1957–74 official published figures were not available in the form required; estimates for these years were obtained from trade sources.

22. Italy

Year ended 30th June	Cigarettes Millions	Cigarettes Mn. lbs.	Cigars Millions	Cigars Mn. lbs.	Cigarillos Millions	Cigarillos Mn. lbs.	Smoking tobacco Mn. lbs.	Snuff Mn. lbs.	Total Mn. lbs.	Population Total Mns.	Population 15+ Mns.	Consumption per adult Cigarettes Number	Consumption per adult Total Lbs.
1921–25 (Average)	11,148	24·6	1,328	14·6	0	0·0	17·1	4·6	60·9	37·9*	26·1*	430	2·3
1926–30 ,,	13,900	30·6	1,188	13·1	29	0·2	17·1	3·8	64·8	39·5*	27·5	510	2·4
1931–35 ,,	12,911	28·5	597	6·6	366	2·0	13·8	2·9	53·8	41·6*	29·0*	450	1·9
1936–40 ,,	17,342	38·2	451	5·0	689	3·8	12·0	2·4	61·4	43·1	30·1	580	2·0
1941–45 ,,	20,748	45·7	468	5·2	527	2·9	12·4	1·6	67·8	44·6	32·1*	650	2·1
1946–50 ,,	22,347	49·3	391	4·3	278	1·5	11·5	1·2	67·8	46·0	33·7	660	2·0
1951–55 ,,	33,978	74·9	420	4·6	75	0·4	11·3	1·2	92·4	47·5	35·1*	970	2·6
1956	40,398	89·1	340	3·7	62	0·3	11·6	1·1	105·8	48·3	36·0*	1,120	2·9
1957	42,658	94·1	326	3·6	55	0·3	11·2	1·1	110·3	48·7*	36·4*	1,170	3·0
1958	44,906	99·0	309	3·4	52	0·3	11·5	1·1	115·3	49·1*	36·8*	1,220	3·1
1959	46,584	102·7	297	3·3	51	0·3	11·6	1·1	119·0	49·6*	37·2*	1,250	3·2
1960	48,313	106·5	289	3·2	52	0·3	11·3	1·0	122·3	50·1*	37·7*	1,280	3·2
1961	51,864	114·4	284	3·1	52	0·3	10·7	1·0	129·5	50·6	38·2	1,360	3·4
1962	55,826	123·1	277	3·1	71	0·4	10·0	0·9	137·5	51·0*	38·5*	1,450	3·6
1963	57,154	126·0	269	3·0	65	0·4	9·4	0·9	139·7	51·3*	38·8*	1,470	3·6
1964	58,599	129·2	263	2·9	72	0·4	9·1	0·8	142·4	51·6*	39·0*	1,500	3·7
Calendar Year													
1965	60,621	133·7	227	2·5	72	0·4	8·4	0·7	145·7	51·9*	39·3*	1,540	3·7
1966	64,645	142·5	232	2·6	73	0·4	7·8	0·6	153·9	52·2*	39·5*	1,640	3·9
1967	66,657	147·0	216	2·4	54	0·3	7·9	0·6	158·2	52·6*	39·7*	1,680	4·0
1968	68,454	150·9	220	2·4	56	0·3	7·5	0·6	161·7	52·9*	40·0*	1,710	4·0
1969	68,563	151·1	215	2·4	49	0·3	7·1	0·5	161·4	53·2*	40·2*	1,710	4·0
1970	69,534	153·3	188	2·1	46	0·3	6·4	0·4	162·5	53·6*	40·5*	1,720	4·0
1971	70,830	156·2	183	2·0	60	0·3	6·0	0·4	164·9	53·9	40·8	1,740	4·0
1972	74,165	163·5	172	1·9	53	0·3	5·4	0·4	171·5	54·3*	41·1*	1,800	4·2
1973	80,131	176·7	158	1·7	50	0·3	5·1	0·3	184·2	54·7*	41·5*	1,930	4·4

Notes

(a) Details of the weight of tobacco consumed by types of product were provided by the Amministrazione dei Monopoli di Stato, Rome. The figures for the years up to 1960 were published in the *Industrial Balance of the Administration*.

(b) The numbers of cigarettes consumed have been estimated from the cigarette consumption in pounds weight by using a conversion factor of 2·205 lbs. per 1,000. The conversion factors used for cigars and cigarillos were 11·025 lbs. per 1,000 and 5·513 lbs. per 1,000 respectively.

(c) Details of the amount of tobacco consumed in individual years before 1956 were not provided. The figures shown above for the years 1921 to 1955 are five-year averages.

(d) A change in the accounting period took place during 1964 when the financial year was converted from a year ended 30th June to a calendar year basis.

44

23. Jamaica

Calendar year	Cigarettes		Cigars		Pipe tobacco	Total	Population		Consumption per adult	
	Millions	Mn. lbs.	Millions	Mn. lbs.	Mn. lbs.	Total Mn. lbs.	Total Mns.	14+ Mns.	Cigarettes Number	Total Lbs.
1963	776	1·7	0	0·0	0·0	1·7	1·7	0·8	970	2·1
1964	1,002	2·3	0	0·0	0·0	2·3	1·7	0·8	1,250	2·9
1965	1,016	2·3	0	0·0	0·0	2·3	1·8	0·8	1,270	2·9
1966	1,074	2·4	0	0·0	0·0	2·4	1·8	0·9	1,190	2·7
1967	1,044	2·3	0	0·0	0·0	2·3	1·8	0·9	1,160	2·6
1968	1,167	2·6	0	0·0	0·0	2·6	1·8	0·9	1,300	2·9
1969	1,140	2·6	0	0·0	0·0	2·6	1·9	0·9	1,270	2·9
1970	1,260	2·8	0	0·0	0·0	2·8	1·9	1·1	1,150	2·5
1971	1,380	3·1	0	0·0	0·0	3·1	1·9	1·1	1,250	2·8
1972	1,570	3·5	0	0·0	0·0	3·5	1·9	1·1	1,430	3·2
1973	1,480	3·3	0	0·0	0·0	3·3	2·0	1·1	1,350	3·0

Notes

(a) Details of the quantities of tobacco products consumed were obtained from the Department of Statistics and from trade sources.

(b) Cigarette consumption in pounds weight has been estimated from the number of cigarettes consumed by using a conversion factor of 2·25 lbs. per 1,000.

(c) Population figures were obtained from the Registrar General and the Department of Statistics.

(d) Consumption per adult figures are based on the population aged 14 years and over.

24. Japan

Year ended 31st March	Cigarettes		Cigars		Fine-cut tobacco	Pipe tobacco	Total	Population		Consumption per adult	
	Millions	Mn. lbs.	Millions	Mn. lbs.	Mn. lbs.	Mn. lbs.	Total Mn. lbs.	Total Mns.	15+ Mns.	Cigarettes Number	Total Lbs.
1920	20,954	46·2	3	0·0	57·8	0·0	104·0	55·4	35·2	600	3·0
1921	22,732	50·1	3	0·0	57·6	0·0	107·7	56·0*	35·6*	640	3·0
1922	24,031	53·0	3	0·0	55·5	0·0	108·5	56·7	36·0*	670	3·0
1923	27,220	60·0	5	0·1	54·3	0·0	114·4	57·5*	36·5*	750	3·1
1924	28,943	63·8	3	0·0	52·4	0·0	116·2	58·3*	36·9*	780	3·1
1925	27,273	60·1	4	0·1	52·1	0·0	112·3	59·2	37·5	730	3·0
1926	27,205	60·0	3	0·0	52·5	0·0	112·5	60·1*	38·0*	720	3·0
1927	29,178	64·3	3	0·0	52·7	0·0	117·0	61·0*	38·6*	760	3·0
1928	30,954	68·3	3	0·0	50·6	0·0	118·9	62·0*	39·2*	790	3·0
1929	31,664	69·8	3	0·0	52·0	0·0	121·8	62·9*	39·8*	800	3·1
1930	30,201	66·6	1	0·0	51·9	0·0	118·5	63·9	40·4	750	2·9
1931	29,368	64·8	1	0·0	50·4	0·0	115·2	64·8*	41·0*	720	2·8
1932	31,831	70·2	1	0·0	51·1	0·0	121·3	65·8	41·6*	770	2·9
1933	33,536	73·9	3	0·0	50·1	0·0	124·0	66·8	42·2*	790	2·9
1934	36,625	80·8	3	0·0	49·0	0·1	129·9	67·7	42·7*	860	3·0
1935	37,907	83·6	3	0·0	47·6	0·0	131·2	68·7	43·3	880	3·0
1936	38,477	84·8	2	0·0	46·1	0·0	130·9	69·6	44·1*	870	3·0
1937	40,641	89·6	1	0·0	47·6	0·0	137·2	70·4	44·6*	910	3·1
1938	40,974	90·3	1	0·0	44·5	0·0	134·8	70·5	44·9*	910	3·0
1939	48,125	106·1	1	0·0	41·0	0·0	147·1	70·9	45·2	1,060	3·3
1940	51,381	113·3	2	0·0	43·2	0·0	156·5	71·4	45·6	1,130	3·4
1941	52,428	115·6	1	0·0	41·3	0·0	156·9	71·6	46·0*	1,140	3·4
1942	53,830	118·7	1	0·0	42·5	0·0	161·2	72·3	46·6*	1,160	3·5
1943	54,258	119·6	0	0·0	41·7	0·0	161·3	73·3	47·5*	1,140	3·4
1944	45,770	100·9	1	0·0	40·8	0·0	141·7	73·8	48·1*	950	2·9
1945	14,691	32·4	0	0·0	36·0	0·0	68·4	72·2	47·3	310	1·4
1946	15,715	34·7	0	0·0	69·8	0·0	104·5	75·8	51·4	310	2·0
1947	17,843	39·3	0	0·0	64·7	0·0	104·0	77·5	50·1	360	2·1
1948	34,263	75·5	3	0·0	49·9	0·5	125·9	79·5	51·9	660	2·4
1949	52,744	116·3	5	0·1	28·9	0·1	145·4	81·3	52·8*	1,000	2·8

Japan (contd)

Year ended 31st March	Cigarettes		Cigars		Fine-cut tobacco	Pipe tobacco	Total	Population		Consumption per adult	
	Millions	Mn. lbs.	Millions	Mn. lbs.	Mn. lbs.	Mn. lbs.	Mn. lbs.	Total Mns.	15 + Mns.	Cigarettes Number	Total Lbs.
1950	65,298	144·0	2	0·0	21·7	0·1	165·8	82·9	53·6	1,220	3·1
1951	73,995	163·2	1	0·0	19·8	0·1	183·1	84·2	54·7	1,350	3·3
1952	80,177	176·8	0	0·0	17·7	0·1	194·6	85·5	55·9	1,430	3·5
1953	89,516	197·4	0	0·0	16·1	0·1	213·6	86·7	57·1*	1,570	3·7
1954	95,614	210·8	0	0·0	15·9	0·1	226·8	88·0	58·4	1,640	3·9
1955	97,646	215·3	0	0·0	14·3	0·1	229·7	89·0	59·3	1,650	3·9
1956	97,212	214·4	1	0·0	12·8	0·1	227·3	90·0	60·7	1,600	3·7
1957	101,403	223·6	1	0·0	11·5	0·1	235·2	90·9	62·1	1,630	3·8
1958	107,405	236·8	1	0·0	10·7	0·1	247·6	92·0	63·5	1,690	3·9
1959	113,196	249·5	1	0·0	9·4	0·1	259·0	92·9	64·9	1,740	4·0
1960	122,760	270·6	1	0·0	8·2	0·1	278·9	93·9	65·3	1,880	4·3
1961	134,431	296·3	1	0·0	6·7	0·1	303·1	94·9	66·2	2,030	4·6
1962	142,013	313·1	2	0·0	5·5	0·1	318·7	95·2	67·9	2,090	4·7
1963	151,111	332·8	1	0·0	4·5	0·1	337·4	96·1	69·7	2,170	4·8
1964	160,807	354·2	1	0·0	3·9	0·1	358·2	97·1	71·5	2,250	5·0
1965	171,449	377·6	1	0·0	3·3	0·1	381·0	98·2	73·1	2,350	5·2
1966	181,488	399·7	2	0·0	3·1	0·1	402·9	99·0	74·5	2,440	5·4
1967	193,932	427·5	3	0·0	2·3	0·2	430·0	100·2	75·8	2,560	5·7
1968	196,709	433·7	2	0·0	2·1	0·2	436·0	101·4	77·0	2,560	5·7
1969	211,316	465·9	2	0·0	1·9	0·1	467·9	102·6	78·0	2,710	6·0
1970	222,132	489·7	2	0·0	1·4	0·1	491·2	103·9	79·1	2,810	6·2
1971	235,449	519·2	2	0·0	0·9	0·1	520·2	105·0	79·8	2,950	6·5
1972	252,665	557·1	2	0·0	0·9	0·2	558·2	107·3	81·4	3,100	6·9
1973	266,692	588·1	2	0·0	0·9	0·2	589·1	108·7	82·3	3,240	7·2

Notes

(a) Details of the number of cigarettes and cigars and of the weight of fine-cut and pipe tobacco consumed were obtained from *Sales of Manufactured Tobaccos Classified by Brands, 1904–1955*, published by the Japan Monopoly Corporation. The figures for 1956 to 1973 were provided by the Japan Monopoly Corporation.

(b) Cigarettes were converted from number to weight using a factor of 2·2c5 lbs. per 1,000 up to 1955. From 1956 onwards details of the numbers and weight of cigarettes consumed were provided by the Japan Monopoly Corporation. The conversion factor used for cigars was 15 lbs. per 1,000.

25. Kenya

Year ended 30th September	Cigarettes		Cigars and cigarillos		Smoking tobacco	Total	Population		Consumption per adult	
	Millions	Mn. lbs.	Millions	Mn. lbs.	Mn. lbs.	Mn. lbs.	Total Mns.	15+ Mns.	Cigarettes Number	Total Lbs.
1964	2,066	4·1	1	0·0	0·1	4·2	9·1	4·9*	420	0·9
1965	1,970	3·9	1	0·0	0·1	4·0	9·4	5·0*	390	0·8
1966	1,964	3·9	1	0·0	0·1	4·0	9·6	5·1*	390	0·8
1967	2,018	4·0	1	0·0	0·1	4·1	9·9	5·2*	390	0·8
1968	2,055	4·1	1	0·0	0·1	4·1	10·2	5·3*	390	0·8
1969	2,096	4·2	1	0·0	0·0	4·2	10·9	5·6	370	0·8
1970	2,326	4·6	2	0·0	0·0	4·7	11·2	5·7*	410	0·8
1971	2,579	5·1	2	0·0	0·0	5·2	11·7	6·0*	430	0·9
1972	2,702	5·4	2	0·0	0·0	5·4	12·1	6·1*	440	0·9
1973	2,977	5·9	2	0·0	0·0	5·9	12·5	6·3*	470	0·9

Notes

(a) Details of the number of cigarettes, cigars and cigarillos and of the weight of smoking tobacco consumed were obtained from trade sources.

(b) Cigarette consumption in pounds weight has been estimated from the number of cigarettes consumed by using a conversion factor of 1·985 lbs. per 1,000. The conversion factor used for cigars and cigarillos was 4·851 lbs. per 1,000.

(c) In addition to the products listed above a small quantity of tobacco, possibly equivalent to 10% of total tobacco consumption, is consumed annually in Kenya in the form of snuff, chewing tobacco and tobacco for hand-rolled cigarettes.

26. Malawi

Calendar year	Cigarettes		Cigars, cheroots and cigarillos		Tobacco for hand-rolled cigarettes and pipe Mn. lbs.	Raw tobacco Mn. lbs.	Snuff Mn. lbs.	Total Mn. lbs.	Population		Consumption per adult	
	Millions	Mn. lbs.	Millions	Mn. lbs.					Total Mns.	15+ Mns.	Cigarettes Number	Total Lbs.
1964	301	0·7	0	0·0	0·0	...	0·0	0·7	3·8	2·1*	140	0·3
1965	337	0·7	0	0·0	0·0	...	0·0	0·8	3·9	2·2*	150	0·3
1966	403	0·9	0	0·0	0·0	...	0·0	0·9	4·0	2·3	180	0·4
1967	433	1·0	0	0·0	0·0	...	0·0	1·0	4·1	2·3*	190	0·4
1968	430	0·9	0	0·0	0·0	...	0·0	1·0	4·2	2·4*	180	0·4
1969	438	1·0	1	0·0	0·0	...	0·0	1·0	4·3	2·4*	180	0·4
1970	450	1·0	0	0·0	0·0	...	0·0	1·0	4·4	2·5*	180	0·4
1971	437	1·0	1	0·0	0·0	...	0·0	1·0	4·6	2·5*	170	0·4
1972	465	1·0	0	0·0	0·0	...	0·0	1·1	4·7	2·6*	180	0·4
1973	541	1·2	1	0·0	0·0	...	0·0	1·2	4·8	2·7*	200	0·5

Notes

(a) Details of the quantities of manufactured tobacco products consumed were obtained from the National Statistical Office of Malawi and from trade sources.

(b) Cigarette consumption in pounds weight has been estimated from the number of cigarettes consumed by using a conversion factor of 2·205 lbs. per 1,000. The conversion factor used for cigars was 6·6 lbs. per 1,000.

(c) An estimated 300,000 lbs. of raw tobacco, which is mainly delivered by small farmers to local markets where it is sold by weight for use in hand-rolled cigarettes, was consumed in 1973.

(d) The sources of the population figures were as follows:
  1964–65 *Economic Report,* 1972, published by the Economic Planning Division of the Office of the President and Cabinet, Zomba.
  1966–73 National Statistical Office of Malawi.

27. Malaysia

Calendar year	Cigarettes		Cigars, cigarillos and cigarlets		Other manufactured tobacco	Total	Population		Consumption per adult	
	Millions	Mn. lbs.	Millions	Mn. lbs.	Mn. lbs.	Mn. lbs.	Total Mns.	15+ Mns.	Cigarettes Number	Total Lbs.
1965	7,450	15·6	3	0·0	0·3	15·9	9·4	5·2*	1,440	3·1
1966	7,242	15·2	3	0·0	0·3	15·5	9·7	5·4*	1,350	2·9
1967	7,243	15·2	4	0·0	0·2	15·5	10·0	5·5*	1,310	2·8
1968	7,521	15·8	5	0·0	0·2	16·0	10·3	5·7*	1,320	2·8
1969	7,843	16·5	4	0·0	0·2	16·7	10·5	5·8*	1,350	2·9
1970	8,161	17·1	3	0·0	0·2	17·4	10·8	6·0*	1,360	2·9
1971	8,492	17·8	3	0·0	0·2	18·0	11·1*	6·2*	1,380	2·9
1972	9,066	19·0	2	0·0	0·2	19·2	11·3*	6·3*	1,440	3·0
1973	10,397	21·8	2	0·0	0·1	22·0	11·6*	6·5*	1,600	3·4

Notes
(a) Details of tobacco consumed by products were obtained from trade sources.
(b) Cigarette consumption in pounds weight has been estimated from the number of cigarettes consumed by using a conversion factor of 2·1 lbs. per 1,000. The conversion factor used for cigars, cigarillos and cigarlets was 6·3 lbs. per 1,000.
(c) Population figures were obtained from the Department of Statistics.

28. Mauritius

Year ended 30th September	Cigarettes Millions	Cigarettes Mn. lbs.	Total Mn. lbs.	Population Total Mns.	Population 15+ Mns.	Consumption per adult Cigarettes Number	Consumption per adult Total Lbs.
1963	647	1·1	1·1	0·7	0·4	1,620	2·8
1964	680	1·2	1·2	0·7	0·4	1,650	2·8
1965	680	1·2	1·2	0·7	0·4	1,610	2·8
1966	693	1·2	1·2	0·7	0·4	1,600	2·8
1967	695	1·2	1·2	0·8	0·4	1,580	2·7
1968	715	1·2	1·2	0·8	0·4	1,590	2·7
1969	715	1·2	1·2	0·8	0·5	1,570	2·7
1970	743	1·3	1·3	0·8	0·5	1,610	2·8
1971	781	1·3	1·3	0·8	0·5	1,670	2·9
1972	822	1·4	1·4	0·8	0·5	1,740	3·0
1973	917	1·6	1·6	0·8	0·5	1,920	3·3

Notes

(a) Details of the numbers of cigarettes consumed were obtained from trade sources. Consumption of cigars and pipe tobacco in Mauritius is negligible.

(b) Cigarette consumption in pounds weight was estimated from the number of cigarettes consumed by using a conversion factor of 1·720 lbs. per 1,000.

(c) Population figures were obtained from Department of Statistics, Government of Mauritius.

29. Mexico

Calendar year	Cigarettes Millions	Mn. lbs.	Cigars Millions	Mn. lbs.	Other manufactured tobacco Mn. lbs.	Total Mn. lbs.	Population Total Mns.	Population 15 + Mns.	Consumption per adult Cigarettes Number	Consumption per adult Total Lbs.
1923	8,240	18·2	13	0·2	...	...	14·8*	9·2*	900	...
1924	7,632	16·8	12	0·2	...	...	15·0*	9·3*	820	...
1925	7,770	17·1	27	0·3	...	...	15·2	9·4*	830	...
1926	9,113	20·1	26	0·3	...	...	15·4*	9·5*	960	...
1927	10,894	24·0	25	0·3	...	...	15·7*	9·6*	1,130	...
1928	10,891	24·0	25	0·3	...	...	16·0*	9·8*	1,110	...
1929	11,635	25·7	23	0·3	0·4	26·4	16·3*	9·9*	1,180	2·7
1930	10,126	22·3	...	...	...	...	16·6	10·1	1,000	...
1931	10,786	23·8	...	...	...	...	16·9*	10·2*	1,060	...
1932	10,731	23·7	...	...	...	...	17·2*	10·4*	1,030	...
1933	12,062	26·6	...	...	...	...	17·5*	10·5*	1,150	...
1934	14,083	31·1	15	0·2	0·1	31·4	17·8*	10·7*	1,320	2·9
1935	15,551	34·3	16	0·2	0·1	34·6	18·1	10·8*	1,440	3·2
1936	16,130	35·6	15	0·2	0·1	35·9	18·4*	11·0*	1,470	3·3
1937	17,908	39·5	16	0·2	0·1	39·8	18·7	11·1*	1,610	3·6
1938	16,993	37·5	19	0·2	0·2	37·9	19·1	11·3*	1,500	3·4
1939	18,914	41·7	18	0·2	0·2	42·1	19·4	11·5*	1,640	3·7
1940	17,938	39·6	18	0·2	0·5	40·3	19·8	11·6	1,550	3·5
1941	17,975	39·6	19	0·2	0·6	40·4	20·3	11·9*	1,510	3·4
1942	19,062	42·0	20	0·2	0·5	42·7	20·9	12·2*	1,560	3·5
1943	18,385	40·5	22	0·3	0·4	41·2	21·4	12·6*	1,460	3·3
1944	22,536	49·7	23	0·3	0·3	50·3	22·0	12·9*	1,750	3·9
1945	20,573	45·4	22	0·3	0·4	46·1	22·6	13·2*	1,560	3·5
1946	23,653	52·2	23	0·3	0·4	52·9	23·2	13·6*	1,740	3·9
1947	21,425	47·2	23	0·4	0·4	47·9	23·8	13·9*	1,540	3·4
1948	21,956	48·4	24	0·3	0·5	49·2	24·5	14·3*	1,540	3·4
1949	23,725	52·3	26	0·3	0·4	53·0	25·1	14·7*	1,610	3·6

Mexico (contd)

Calendar year	Cigarettes		Cigars		Other manufactured tobacco	Total	Population		Consumption per adult	
	Millions	Mn. lbs.	Millions	Mn. lbs.	Mn. lbs.	Mn. lbs.	Total Mns.	15+ Mns.	Cigarettes Number	Total Lbs.
1950	22,734	50·1	25	0·3	0·5	50·9	25·8	15·1	1,510	3·4
1951	24,274	53·5	29	0·4	0·4	54·3	26·5	15·4*	1,580	3·5
1952	24,540	54·1	29	0·4	0·3	54·8	27·3	15·9*	1,540	3·4
1953	25,006	55·1	28	0·4	0·4	55·9	28·1	16·3*	1,530	3·4
1954	25,887	57·1	30	0·4	0·4	57·9	28·9	16·8*	1,540	3·4
1955	27,355	60·3	33	0·4	0·6	61·3	29·7	17·2*	1,590	3·6
1956	28,208	62·2	33	0·4	0·5	63·1	30·5	17·9*	1,580	3·5
1957	29,148	64·3	34	0·4	0·4	65·1	31·4	18·4*	1,580	3·5
1958	30,653	67·6	34	0·4	0·1	68·1	32·3	18·9*	1,620	3·6
1959	31,744	70·0	37	0·5	0·0	70·5	33·3	19·5*	1,630	3·6
1960	33,191	73·2	39	0·5	0·0	73·7	35·0	19·5	1,700	3·8
1961	33,156	73·1	34	0·4	0·1	73·6	36·1	20·1*	1,650	3·7
1962	32,355	71·3	37	0·5	0·1	71·9	37·2	20·8*	1,560	3·5
1963	32,816	72·4	35	0·5	0·1	73·0	38·4	21·4*	1,530	3·4
1964	33,483	73·8	36	0·5	0·1	74·4	39·6	22·1*	1,520	3·4
1965	34,408	75·9	37	0·5	0·2	76·6	40·8	22·8*	1,510	3·4
1966	35,711	78·7	37	0·5	0·2	79·4	42·3	23·4*	1,530	3·4
1967	35,716	78·8	38	0·5	0·1	79·4	43·8	24·0*	1,490	3·3
1968	38,106	84·0	36	0·5	0·1	84·6	45·3	24·6*	1,550	3·4
1969	39,046	86·1	34	0·4	0·1	86·6	46·8	25·3*	1,540	3·4
1970	41,523	91·6	33	0·4	0·1	92·1	48·4	26·0	1,600	3·5
1971	40,746	89·8	33	0·4	0·1	90·3	50·4	27·1	1,500	3·3
1972	44,531	98·2	33	0·4	0·1	98·7	52·5	28·2	1,580	3·5
1973	39,958	88·1	32	0·4	0·1	88·6	54·5	29·3	1,360	3·0

Notes

(a) Details of the numbers of cigarettes and cigars and of the weight of other manufactured tobacco consumed were obtained from trade sources in Mexico.

(b) Cigarette consumption in pounds weight has been estimated from the number of cigarettes consumed by using a conversion factor of 2·205 lbs. per 1,000. The conversion factor used for cigars was 12·5 lbs. per 1,000.

(c) Population figures from 1960 to 1965 were taken from *Guia de los Mercados de Mexico*. From 1966 onwards the figures were obtained from the Census Office of the Mexican Ministry of Industry and Commerce.

30. Morocco

Calendar year	Cigarettes Millions	Cigarettes Mn. lbs.	Cigars Millions	Cigars Mn. lbs.	Smoking tobacco Mn. lbs.	Snuff Mn. lbs.	Total Mn. lbs.	Population Total Mns.	Population 15+ Mns.	Consumption per adult Cigarettes Number	Consumption per adult Total Lbs.
1934	1,044	2·3	3	0·0	1·1	0·5	3·9	7·0	4·2	250	0·9
1935	1,003	2·2	3	0·0	1·0	0·5	3·7	7·0	4·2	240	0·9
1936	978	2·2	3	0·0	1·1	0·5	3·8	7·1	4·3	230	0·9
1937	999	2·2	3	0·0	1·1	0·5	3·8	7·2	4·3	230	0·9
1938	1,122	2·5	3	0·0	1·0	0·5	4·0	7·3	4·4	250	0·9
1939	1,199	2·7	3	0·0	1·0	0·5	4·2	7·5	4·5	270	0·9
1940	1,511	3·4	2	0·0	1·1	0·6	5·1	7·6	4·5	330	1·1
1941	1,691	3·8	2	0·0	1·3	0·6	5·7	7·7	4·6	370	1·2
1942	1,653	3·6	1	0·0	1·4	0·6	5·6	7·8	4·7	360	1·2
1943	1,624	3·6	2	0·0	1·3	0·7	5·6	7·8	4·7	350	1·2
1944	1,657	3·7	2	0·0	0·8	0·8	5·3	7·9	4·8	350	1·1
1945	1,702	3·8	2	0·0	0·8	0·8	5·4	8·1	4·8	360	1·1
1946	1,997	4·4	2	0·0	0·8	0·7	5·9	8·2	4·8	410	1·2
1947	2,328	5·1	2	0·0	0·7	0·8	6·6	8·3	4·9	470	1·3
1948	2,620	5·8	2	0·0	0·6	0·7	7·1	8·5	5·0	520	1·4
1949	2,475	5·5	1	0·0	0·5	0·8	6·8	8·7	5·1	480	1·3
1950	2,640	5·8	2	0·0	0·7	0·9	7·4	8·9	5·1	510	1·4
1951	2,771	6·1	3	0·0	0·9	0·9	7·9	9·1	5·3	520	1·5
1952	3,097	6·8	4	0·0	0·9	0·9	8·6	9·3	5·4	570	1·6
1953	3,373	7·4	4	0·0	1·0	0·8	9·2	9·6	5·6	600	1·6
1954	2,979	6·6	3	0·0	0·9	0·8	8·3	9·9	5·8	520	1·4
1955	2,964	6·5	4	0·0	0·9	0·8	8·2	10·2	5·8	510	1·4
1956	3,762	8·3	5	0·0	1·0	0·7	10·0	10·5	6·0	630	1·7
1957	3,509	7·7	3	0·0	1·0	0·8	9·5	10·9	6·2	570	1·5
1958	3,470	7·7	3	0·0	1·1	0·8	9·6	11·1	6·3	550	1·5
1959	3,327	7·4	2	0·0	1·1	0·8	9·3	11·4	6·4	520	1·5

Morocco (contd)

Calendar year	Cigarettes Millions	Cigarettes Mn. lbs.	Cigars Millions	Cigars Mn. lbs.	Smoking tobacco Mn. lbs.	Snuff Mn. lbs.	Total Mn. lbs.	Population Total Mns.	Population 15+ Mns.	Consumption per adult Cigarettes Number	Consumption per adult Total Lbs.
1960	3,679	8·1	2	0·0	1·5	0·8	10·4	11·6	6·5	570	1·6
1961	3,880	8·5	2	0·0	1·5	0·8	10·8	12·0	6·5	600	1·7
1962	3,953	8·7	2	0·0	1·5	0·8	11·0	12·3	6·6	590	1·7
1963	4,298	9·5	2	0·0	1·6	0·8	11·9	12·6	6·8	630	1·7
1964	4,194	9·3	1	0·0	1·7	0·8	11·8	13·0	7·0	600	1·7
1965	4,073	9·0	1	0·0	1·9	0·8	11·7	13·3	7·2	570	1·6
1966	4,198	9·3	1	0·0	1·8	0·8	11·9	13·6	7·4	570	1·6
1967	4,214	9·3	2	0·0	1·8	0·8	11·9	14·0	7·6	560	1·6
1968	4,607	10·2	2	0·0	1·9	0·8	12·9	14·3	7·7	590	1·7
1969	4,758	10·5	2	0·0	1·8	0·9	13·2	14·8	8·0	600	1·7
1970	5,133	11·3	2	0·0	1·9	0·9	14·1	15·2	8·2	620	1·7
1971	5,369	11·8	3	0·0	2·5	0·1	14·5	15·6	8·4	640	1·7
1972	5,927	13·1	3	0·0	2·3	0·1	15·5	16·0	8·6	690	1·8

Notes
(a) Details of the weights of cigarettes, cigars, smoking tobacco and snuff consumed were provided by the Regie des Tabacs, Casablanca.
(b) The numbers of cigarettes consumed have been estimated from the cigarette consumption in pounds weight by using a conversion factor of 2·205 lbs. per 1,000. The conversion factor for cigars is 6·615 lbs. per 1,000.

31. Netherlands

Calendar year	Cigarettes		Cigars		Cigarillos		Cut tobacco	Total	Population		Consumption per adult	
	Millions	Mn. lbs.	Millions	Mn. lbs.	Millions	Mn. lbs.	Mn. lbs.	Mn. lbs.	Total Mns.	15+ Mns.	Cigarettes Number	Total Lbs.
1923	1,958	4·3	1,043	13·1			28·0	45·4	7·1	4·8	410	9·5
1924	2,507	5·5	1,037	13·1			32·2	50·8	7·3	4·9	510	10·4
1925	1,982	4·4	1,063	13·4	Combined with cigars		23·4	41·2	7·4	5·0	400	8·2
1926	2,369	5·2	1,145	14·4			27·7	47·3	7·5	5·1	460	9·3
1927	2,591	5·7	1,198	15·1			26·1	46·9	7·6	5·2	500	9·0
1928	2,791	6·2	1,267	16·0			25·9	48·1	7·7	5·3	530	9·1
1929	3,180	7·0	1,346	17·0			24·9	48·9	7·8	5·4	590	9·1
1930	3,590	7·9	1,370	17·3			25·5	50·7	7·9	5·5	650	9·2
1931	3,554	7·8	1,369	17·2			27·1	52·1	8·0	5·6	630	9·3
1932	3,655	8·1	1,355	17·1			28·5	53·7	8·1	5·7	640	9·4
1933	3,914	8·6	1,409	17·8			28·1	54·5	8·2	5·8	670	9·4
1934	3,926	8·7	1,015	15·2	414	2·1	23·2	49·2	8·3	5·9	670	8·3
1935	4,009	8·8	1,048	15·7	380	1·9	23·3	49·7	8·4	5·9	680	8·4
1936	3,969	8·8	1,116	16·7	353	1·8	24·2	51·5	8·5	6·0	660	8·6
1937	4,349	9·6	1,185	17·8	314	1·6	23·8	52·8	8·6	6·1	710	8·7
1938	4,766	10·5	1,238	18·6	311	1·6	22·2	52·9	8·7	6·2	770	8·5
1939	5,234	11·5	1,338	20·1	340	1·7	25·1	58·4	8·8	6·3	830	9·3
1946	3,332	7·3	525	7·9	264	1·3	10·4	26·9	9·4	6·8	490	4·0
1947	5,362	11·8	626	9·4	278	1·4	17·7	40·3	9·6	6·9	780	5·8
1948	5,334	11·8	673	10·1	211	1·1	19·7	42·7	9·8	7·0	760	6·1
1949	6,092	13·4	745	11·2	181	0·9	24·8	50·3	10·0	7·1	860	7·1
1950	8,048	17·7	655	9·8	134	0·7	25·8	54·0	10·1	7·2	1,120	7·5
1951	8,442	18·6	594	8·9	123	0·6	23·4	51·5	10·3	7·2	1,170	7·2
1952	9,472	20·9	690	10·4	121	0·6	23·0	54·9	10·4	7·3	1,300	7·5
1953	10,134	22·3	783	11·7	112	0·6	22·1	56·7	10·5	7·4	1,370	7·7
1954	11,296	24·9	850	12·8	145	0·7	21·8	60·2	10·6	7·4	1,530	8·1

Netherlands (contd)

Calendar year	Cigarettes Millions	Cigarettes Mn. lbs.	Cigars Millions	Cigars Mn. lbs.	Cigarillos Millions	Cigarillos Mn. lbs.	Cut tobacco Mn. lbs.	Total Mn. lbs.	Population Total Mns.	Population 15+ Mns.	Consumption per adult Cigarettes Number	Consumption per adult Total Lbs.
1955	11,734	25·9	906	13·6	150	0·8	18·3	58·6	10·8	7·5	1,560	7·8
1956	13,149	29·0	942	14·1	151	0·8	18·1	62·0	10·9	7·6	1,730	8·2
1957	13,457	29·7	967	14·5	195	1·0	17·9	63·1	11·0	7·7*	1,750	8·2
1958	13,043	28·8	968	14·5	202	1·0	19·6	63·9	11·3	7·9	1,650	8·1
1959	13,452	29·7	1,016	15·2	244	1·2	20·7	66·8	11·4	8·0	1,680	8·4
1960	13,753	30·3	1,074	16·1	299	1·5	21·0	68·9	11·6	8·1	1,700	8·5
1961	14,635	32·3	1,148	17·2	299	1·5	21·3	72·3	11·7	8·3	1,760	8·7
1962	15,190	33·5	1,107	16·6	319	1·6	20·3	72·0	11·9	8·4	1,810	8·6
1963	16,297	35·9	1,223	18·3	389	1·9	20·9	77·0	12·0	8·6	1,900	9·0
1964	14,073	31·0	1,142	17·1	479	2·4	21·8	72·3	12·2	8·7	1,620	8·3
1965	17,950	39·6	1,126	16·9	409	2·0	24·7	83·2	12·4	8·9	2,020	9·3
1966	14,201	31·3	1,100	16·5	401	2·0	23·1	72·9	12·5	9·0	1,580	8·1
1967	16,647	36·7	1,068	16·0	363	1·8	25·0	79·5	12·6	9·1*	1,830	8·7
1968	18,497	40·8	1,096	16·4	403	2·0	26·2	85·4	12·8	9·3	1,990	9·2
1969	16,251	35·8	955	14·3	342	1·7	25·8	77·6	13·0	9·4	1,730	8·3
1970	18,675	41·2	1,058	15·9	354	1·8	26·0	84·9	13·1	9·5*	1,970	8·9
1971	19,559	43·1	937	14·1	371	1·9	25·9	85·0	13·2*	9·6*	2,040	8·9
1972	21,660	47·8	903	13·5	338	1·7	27·8	90·8	13·4	9·8	2,210	9·3
1973	23,423	51·6	930	14·0	334	1·7	29·6	96·9	13·5	9·9	2,370	9·8

Notes

(a) Details of the number of cigarettes, cigars and cigarillos and of the weight of cut tobacco consumed were obtained from *Produktiestatistieken Tabakverwerkende Industrie*, 1956, published by the Netherlands Central Bureau of Statistics and *Statistics of Banderoles Issued*, published by the Stichting Tabakverwerkende Industrie.

(b) Cigarette consumption in pounds weight has been estimated from the number of cigarettes consumed by using a conversion factor of 2·205 lbs. per 1,000. The conversion factors used for cigars and cigarillos were 15 lbs. per 1,000 and 5 lbs. per 1,000 respectively.

(c) The source of the figures of tobacco consumption given above also provides information for the years 1940–45. These years have been omitted from the table above, however, as, according to the Central Bureau of Statistics, the figures are quite unreliable.

(d) The sources of the population figures were as follows:
1923–52 *Bevolking van Nederland; Leeftijd en Geslacht*, 1953–73 *Maandstatistiek van de Bevolking* and *Statistisch Zakboek*, all published by the Netherlands Central Bureau of Statistics.

32. New Zealand

Calendar year	Cigarettes		Tobacco for hand-rolled cigarettes and pipe	Total	Population		Consumption per adult	
	Millions	Mn. lbs.	Mn. lbs.	Mn. lbs.	Total Mns.	15+ Mns.	Cigarettes Number	Total Lbs.
1920	511	1·3	3·1	4·4	1·2	0·8*	640	5·5
1921	392	1·0	2·7	3·7	1·3	0·9	440	4·1
1922	443	1·1	2·6	3·7	1·3*	0·9*	490	4·1
1923	495	1·2	2·6	3·8	1·3*	0·9*	550	4·2
1924	542	1·4	2·6	4·0	1·4*	0·9	600	4·4
1925	606	1·5	3·0	4·5	1·4	1·0*	610	4·5
1926	645	1·6	2·9	4·5	1·4	1·0*	650	4·5
1927	686	1·7	3·1	4·8	1·4*	1·0*	690	4·8
1928	683	1·7	3·0	4·7	1·5	1·0*	680	4·7
1929	719	1·8	3·2	5·0	1·5*	1·0	720	5·0
1930	626	1·6	3·3	4·9	1·5	1·1*	570	4·5
1931	498	1·2	3·4	4·6	1·5*	1·1*	450	4·2
1932	406	1·0	3·4	4·4	1·5	1·1*	370	4·0
1933	426	1·1	3·4	4·5	1·5	1·1*	390	4·1
1934	463	1·2	3·5	4·7	1·6	1·1*	420	4·3
1935	584	1·5	3·4	4·9	1·6	1·1	530	4·5
1936	712	1·8	3·7	5·5	1·6	1·2	590	4·6
1937	828	2·1	3·8	5·9	1·6	1·2*	690	4·9
1938	916	2·3	3·9	6·2	1·6	1·2	760	5·2
1939	943	2·4	4·2	6·6	1·6	1·2	790	5·5
1940	852	2·1	4·2	6·3	1·6	1·2*	710	5·3
1941	900	2·3	4·3	6·6	1·6	1·2*	750	5·5
1942	1,000	2·5	3·8	6·3	1·6	1·2*	830	5·3
1943	1,018	2·5	3·4	5·9	1·6	1·2	850	4·9
1944	1,134	2·8	3·2	6·0	1·7	1·2*	950	5·0
1945	1,180	3·0	3·6	6·6	1·7	1·2	980	5·5
1946	1,582	4·0	4·1	8·1	1·8	1·3*	1,220	6·2
1947	2,044	5·1	4·1	9·2	1·8	1·3*	1,570	7·1
1948	1,682	4·2	4·4	8·6	1·8	1·3	1,290	6·6
1949	1,714	4·3	4·4	8·7	1·9	1·3	1,320	6·7

New Zealand (*contd*)

Calendar year	Cigarettes		Tobacco for hand-rolled cigarettes and pipe	Total	Population		Consumption per adult	
	Millions	Mn. lbs.	Mn. lbs.	Mn. lbs.	Total Mns.	15 + Mns.	Cigarettes Number	Total Lbs.
1950	1,984	5·0	5·1	10·1	1·9	1·4	1,420	7·2
1951	2,152	5·4	5·2	10·6	1·9	1·4	1,540	7·6
1952	2,080	5·2	5·2	10·4	2·0	1·4	1,490	7·4
1953	2,091	5·2	5·5	10·7	2·0	1·4	1,490	7·6
1954	2,306	5·8	5·4	11·2	2·1	1·4	1,650	8·0
1955	2,567	6·4	5·2	11·6	2·1	1·5	1,710	7·7
1956	2,629	6·6	4·5	11·1	2·2	1·5	1,750	7·4
1957	2,792	7·0	4·9	11·9	2·2	1·5	1,860	7·9
1958	2,606	6·5	4·7	11·2	2·3	1·5	1,740	7·5
1959	2,509	6·3	4·7	11·0	2·3	1·5	1,670	7·3
1960	3,082	7·7	4·8	12·5	2·4	1·6	1,930	7·8
1961	3,191	7·9	4·8	12·7	2·5	1·6	1,990	7·9
1962	3,383	8·4	4·5	12·9	2·5	1·6	2,110	8·1
1963	3,703	9·3	4·4	13·7	2·5	1·7	2,180	8·1
1964	3,796	9·5	3·9	13·4	2·6	1·7	2,230	7·9
1965	4,102	10·3	3·4	13·7	2·6	1·8	2,280	7·6
1966	4,557	11·4	3·2	14·6	2·7	1·8	2,530	8·1
1967	4,542	11·4	2·8	14·2	2·7	1·9	2,390	7·5
1968	4,649	11·6	2·6	14·2	2·7	1·9	2,450	7·5
1969	4,818	12·0	2·4	14·4	2·8	1·9	2,540	7·6
1970	4,952	12·4	2·3	14·7	2·8	1·9	2,610	7·7
1971	5,118	12·8	2·1	14·9	2·9	1·9	2,690	7·8
1972	5,405	13·5	2·1	15·6	3·0	2·1	2,570	7·4
1973	5,525	13·8	1·9	15·7	3·0	2·2	2,510	7·1

Notes
(*a*) Details of the weight of cigarettes and tobacco consumed were provided by the New Zealand Department of Statistics, Wellington.
(*b*) A factor of 2·5 lbs. per 1,000 cigarettes, provided by the New Zealand Department of Statistics, was used for converting the weight of cigarettes consumed to numbers.

32(a). New Zealand

Releases from bond of cigarette papers

Calendar year	Produced in New Zealand Millions	Imported Millions
1935	77	1,273
1936	77	1,512
1937	83	1,434
1938	98	1,882
1939	222	1,254
1940	1,751	57
1941	1,842	1
1942	1,666	4
1943	1,899	—
1944	1,656	—
1945	1,596	1
1946	1,395	60
1947	1,772	1,509
1948	2,052	103
1949	1,875	—
1950	2,232	151
1951	2,218	—
1952	2,715	67
1953	2,340	—
1954	2,282	—
1955	2,171	82
1956	2,373	450
1957	2,202	1
1958	2,286	1
1959	2,405	137
1960	2,366	11
1961	2,228	—
1962	2,070	—
1963	1,971	—
1964	1,680	—
1965	1,487	—
1966	1,324	—
1967	1,178	—
1968	1,125	—
1969	985	—
1970	911	—
1971	810	—
1972	1,000	—
1973	857	—

The figures above show releases from bond of cigarette papers and tubes subject to Customs and Excise duties. These figures exclude cigarette paper for use in factory manufacture. This data provides an indication of the extent of the hand-rolling of cigarettes in New Zealand, but the retail sales do not, of course, take account of subsequent wastage.

33. Nicaragua

Calendar year	Cigarettes Millions	Mn. lbs.	Total Mn. lbs.	Population Total Mns.	15+ Mns.	Consumption per adult Cigarettes Number	Total Lbs.
1965	935	1·9	1·9	1·7*	0·8*	1,140	2·3
1966	985	2·0	2·0	1·7*	0·8*	1,170	2·3
1967	1,115	2·2	2·2	1·8*	0·9*	1,300	2·6
1968	1,168	2·3	2·3	1·8*	0·9*	1,310	2·6
1969	1,128	2·3	2·3	1·9*	0·9*	1,240	2·5
1970	1,330	2·4	2·4	1·9*	0·9*	1,410	2·5
1971	1,389	2·5	2·5	2·0	1·0*	1,430	2·6
1972	1,419	2·6	2·6	2·1*	1·0*	1,420	2·6
1973	1,565	2·8	2·8	2·1*	1·0*	1,520	2·7
1974	1,752	3·2	3·2	2·2*	1·1*	1,650	3·0

Notes

(a) Details of the numbers of cigarettes consumed were obtained from trade sources.

(b) Cigarette consumption in pounds weight was estimated from the number of cigarettes consumed by using a conversion factor of 2·0 lbs. per 1,000 for the years up to 1969. From 1970 onwards a conversion factor of 1·8 lbs. per 1,000 was used.

(c) Consumption of other manufactured tobacco goods in Nicaragua is negligible.

34. Norway

Calendar year	Cigarettes		Cigars		Tobacco for hand-rolled cigarettes and pipe	Chewing tobacco	Snuff	Total	Population		Consumption per adult	
	Millions	Mn. lbs.	Millions	Mn. lbs.	Mn. lbs.	Mn. lbs.	Mn. lbs.	Total Mn. lbs.	Total Mns.	15+ Mns.	Cigarettes Number	Total Lbs.
1927	512	1·2	21	0·2	2·1	2·1	1·0	6·6	2·8	2·0*	260	3·3
1928	510	1·2	22	0·2	2·2	2·1	1·0	6·7	2·8	2·0*	260	3·4
1929	545	1·4	21	0·2	2·3	2·1	1·1	7·1	2·8	2·0*	270	3·6
1930	615	1·6	23	0·2	2·4	2·0	1·0	7·2	2·8	2·0	310	3·6
1931	551	1·4	20	0·1	2·5	1·8	0·9	6·7	2·8	2·0*	280	3·4
1932	568	1·4	20	0·1	2·5	1·7	0·9	6·6	2·8	2·1*	270	3·1
1933	583	1·5	20	0·1	2·6	1·5	0·9	6·6	2·9	2·1*	280	3·1
1934	619	1·6	23	0·2	2·7	1·5	0·9	6·9	2·9	2·1*	290	3·3
1935	651	1·6	25	0·2	2·9	1·4	0·9	7·0	2·9	2·2	300	3·2
1936	731	1·8	26	0·2	3·1	1·4	0·9	7·4	2·9	2·2	330	3·4
1937	841	2·1	30	0·2	3·2	1·3	1·0	7·8	2·9	2·2*	380	3·5
1938	833	2·1	31	0·2	3·3	1·3	1·0	7·9	2·9	2·3	360	3·4
1939	909	2·3	31	0·2	3·7	1·3	1·0	8·5	3·0	2·3	400	3·7
1940	973	2·5	31	0·2	3·8	1·2	1·2	8·9	3·0	2·3*	420	3·9
1941	725	1·8	21	0·1	2·7	0·8	1·2	6·6	3·0	2·3*	320	2·9
1942	608	1·5	12	0·1	1·9	0·7	1·0	5·2	3·0	2·3*	260	2·3
1943	562	1·5	7	0·0	1·5	0·5	0·8	4·3	3·0	2·4*	230	1·8
1944	358	0·9	5	0·0	1·3	0·4	0·6	3·2	3·1	2·4*	150	1·3
1945	517	1·3	5	0·0	1·9	0·4	0·6	4·2	3·1	2·4	220	1·8
1946	1,288	3·3	14	0·1	4·7	1·2	1·1	10·4	3·1	2·4	540	4·3
1947	1,548	4·1	22	0·1	5·2	0·9	1·1	11·4	3·2	2·4*	650	4·8
1948	1,506	4·0	21	0·1	5·2	1·0	1·2	11·5	3·2	2·5	600	4·6
1949	1,396	3·7	22	0·1	5·3	0·8	1·2	11·1	3·2	2·5	560	4·4

Norway (contd)

Calendar year	Cigarettes		Cigars		Cigarlets	Tobacco for hand-rolled cigarettes and pipe	Chewing tobacco	Snuff	Total	Population		Consumption per adult	
	Millions	Mn. lbs.	Millions	Mn. lbs.	Millions	Mn. lbs.	Mn. lbs.	Mn. lbs.	Total Mn. lbs.	Total Mns.	15 + Mns.	Cigarettes Number	Total Lbs.
1950	1,280	3·4	18	0·1		5·3	0·7	1·2	10·7	3·3	2·5	510	4·3
1951	1,232	3·2	16	0·1		5·4	0·7	1·2	10·6	3·3	2·5	490	4·2
1952	1,344	3·6	17	0·1		5·7	0·6	1·2	11·2	3·3	2·5	540	4·5
1953	1,305	3·4	21	0·1		5·8	0·6	1·2	11·1	3·4	2·5	520	4·4
1954	1,339	3·5	23	0·1		5·6	0·6	1·2	11·0	3·4	2·5	540	4·4
1955	1,427	3·5	21	0·1		5·8	0·5	1·2	11·1	3·4	2·5	570	4·4
1956	1,340	3·2	21	0·1		5·7	0·5	1·2	10·7	3·5	2·6	520	4·1
1957	1,441	3·5	24	0·1		6·0	0·5	1·1	11·2	3·5	2·6	550	4·3
1958	1,394	3·4	25	0·1		6·3	0·5	1·1	11·4	3·5	2·6	540	4·4
1959	1,420	3·4	26	0·1		6·6	0·4	1·1	11·6	3·5	2·6	550	4·5
1960	1,491	3·6	26	0·1		6·9	0·4	1·0	12·0	3·6	2·7	550	4·4
1961	1,424	3·5	34	0·2		7·4	0·4	1·0	12·5	3·6	2·7	530	4·6
1962	1,464	3·6	37	0·2		7·7	0·4	1·0	12·9	3·6	2·7	540	4·8
1963	1,403	3·4	41	0·2		7·7	0·3	1·0	12·6	3·7	2·7	520	4·7
1964	1,280	3·2	59	0·3		7·8	0·3	1·0	12·6	3·7	2·8	460	4·5
1965	1,462	3·6	50	0·2		8·2	0·3	0·9	13·2	3·7	2·8	520	4·7
1966	1,506	3·7	50*	0·2		8·6	0·3	0·9	13·7	3·7	2·8	540	4·9
1967	1,624	3·9	55*	0·3		8·8	0·2	0·8	14·0	3·7	2·8	580	5·0
1968	1,773	4·3	55*	0·3		8·8	0·2	0·9	14·5	3·8	2·8	630	5·2
1969	1,917	4·6	55*	0·3		9·3	0·2	0·6	15·0	3·8	2·8	690	5·4
1970	1,831	4·4	45*	0·2	30*	8·9	0·2	0·7	14·4	3·9	2·9	630	5·0
1971	1,752	4·2	55	0·2	20	8·8	0·2	0·7	14·1	3·9	2·9	600	4·9
1972	1,862	4·5	54	0·2	18	9·5	0·2	0·7	15·0	3·9	2·9	640	5·2
1973	1,842	4·4	53	0·2	15	9·6	0·2	0·6	15·0	3·9	2·9	640	5·2

Notes

(a) Details of the number and weight of cigarettes and cigars and of the weight of smoking tobacco, chewing tobacco and snuff consumed were obtained from Tobakkindustriens Felleskontor, Oslo. The sources used were *Norges Industri* for details of production, and *Norges Hamdel* for import statistics, both published by the Central Bureau of Statistics of Norway.

(b) The population figures were obtained from the Central Bureau of Statistics of Norway.

35. Pakistan

Year ended 31st March	Cigarettes		Biris		Hookah tobacco	Total	Population		Consumption per adult	
	Millions	Mn. lbs.	Millions	Mn. lbs.	Mn. lbs.	Mn. lbs.	Total Mns.	15+ Mns.	Cigarettes Number	Total Lbs.
1964	11,476	28·7	4,277	5·6	59·4	93·7	48·8	25·2	460	3·7
1965	11,686	29·2	4,865	6·3	60·0	95·6	50·6	26·0	450	3·7
1966	14,000	35·0	3,717	4·8	60·6	100·4	52·4	26·9	520	3·7
1967	17,261	43·2	1,953	2·5	61·2	106·9	54·3	27·8	620	3·8
1968	17,963	44·9	2,521	3·3	61·8	110·0	56·3	28·8	620	3·8
1969	18,843	47·1	2,767	3·6	62·4	113·1	58·3	29·8	630	3·8
1970	21,128	52·8	1,748	2·3	63·0	118·1	60·4	30·8	690	3·8
1971	21,354	53·4	2,770	3·6	63·6	120·6	62·6	31·9	670	3·8
1972	21,642	54·1	2,294	3·0	64·2	121·3	64·9	33·0	660	3·7
1973	25,868	64·7	1,186	1·5	64·9	131·1	67·2	34·2	760	3·8

Notes

(a) Details of the numbers of cigarettes consumed were obtained from Central Excise and Land Customs, Government of Pakistan. Details of the consumption of biris and hookah tobacco were obtained from trade sources.

(b) Cigarette consumption in pounds weight has been estimated from the number of cigarettes consumed by using a conversion factor of 2·5 lbs. per 1,000. The conversion factor used for biris was 1·3 lbs. per 1,000.

(c) Consumption of smoking tobacco, chewing tobacco and snuff in Pakistan is negligible.

36. Portugal

Calendar year	Cigarettes		Cigars and cigarillos		Tobacco for hand-rolled cigarettes and pipe	Snuff	Total	Population		Consumption per adult	
	Millions	Mn. lbs.	Millions	Mn. lbs.	Mn. lbs.	Mn. lbs.	Total Mn. lbs.	Total Mns.	15+ Mns.	Cigarettes Number	Total Lbs.
1940	1,428	3·1	6	0·1	3·9	0·1	7·2	7·7	5·3	270	1·4
1941	1,716	3·8	6	0·1	4·2	0·1	8·2	7·8	5·3*	320	1·5
1942	2,170	4·8	9	0·1	4·4	0·1	9·4	7·8	5·4*	400	1·7
1943	2,251	5·0	10	0·1	4·2	0·1	9·4	7·9	5·4*	420	1·7
1944	2,305	5·1	10	0·1	4·6	0·1	9·9	8·0	5·5*	420	1·8
1945	2,411	5·3	7	0·1	4·8	0·1	10·3	8·0	5·6*	430	1·8
1946	2,626	5·8	3	0·0	4·8	0·1	10·7	8·1	5·7*	460	1·9
1947	3,161	7·0	2	0·0	3·9	0·1	11·0	8·2	5·7	550	1·9
1948	3,343	7·4	1	0·0	4·5	0·1	12·0	8·3	5·8*	580	2·1
1949	3,573	7·9	2	0·0	3·6	0·1	11·6	8·3	5·9	610	2·0
1950	3,633	8·0	1	0·0	3·2	0·1	11·3	8·4	5·9	620	1·9
1951	3,802	8·4	1	0·0	3·2	0·1	11·7	8·5	6·0	630	2·0
1952	4,183	9·2	1	0·0	3·2	0·1	12·5	8·5	6·0	700	2·1
1953	4,215	9·3	1	0·0	2·9	0·1	12·3	8·5	6·1	690	2·0
1954	4,317	9·5	2	0·0	2·6	0·0	12·1	8·6	6·1	710	2·0
1955	4,674	10·3	2	0·0	2·4	0·0	12·7	8·6	6·1	770	2·1
1956	5,100	11·2	2	0·0	2·1	0·0	13·3	8·7	6·2	820	2·1
1957	5,088	11·2	2	0·0	1·8	0·1	13·1	8·7	6·2	820	2·1
1958	5,510	12·1	2	0·0	1·8	0·0	13·9	8·7	6·2	890	2·2
1959	5,778	12·7	2	0·0	1·7	0·0	14·4	8·8	6·2	930	2·3
1960	6,287	13·9	1	0·0	1·6	0·0	15·5	8·9	6·3	1,000	2·5
1961	5,570	12·3	1	0·0	1·5	0·0	13·8	9·0*	6·4*	870	2·2
1962	5,827	12·8	2	0·0	1·6	0·0	14·4	9·1*	6·4*	910	2·3
1963	6,757	14·9	1	0·0	1·6	0·0	16·5	9·2*	6·5*	1,040	2·5
1964	7,029	15·5	1	0·0	1·8	0·0	17·3	9·2*	6·6*	1,070	2·6

Portugal (contd)

Calendar year	Cigarettes		Cigars and cigarillos		Tobacco for hand-rolled cigarettes and pipe Mn. lbs.	Snuff Mn. lbs.	Total Mn. lbs.	Population		Consumption per adult	
	Millions	Mn. lbs.	Millions	Mn. lbs.				Total Mns.	15 + Mns.	Cigarettes Number	Total Lbs.
1965	7,482	16·5	1	0·0	1·2	0·0	17·7	9·2*	6·6*	1,130	2·7
1966	7,989	17·7	1	0·0	1·2	0·0	18·9	9·2*	6·6*	1,210	2·9
1967	8,237	18·2	2	0·0	1·1	0·0	19·3	9·2*	6·5*	1,270	3·0
1968	8,820	19·5	2	0·0	1·0	0·0	20·5	9·1*	6·5*	1,360	3·2
1969	8,689	19·2	1	0·0	1·0	0·0	20·2	9·1*	6·5*	1,340	3·1
1970	8,924	19·7	1	0·0	0·8	0·0	20·6	9·0*	6·4*	1,390	3·2
1971	9,082	20·0	1	0·0	0·8	0·0	20·9	8·9*	6·4*	1,420	3·3
1972	9,406	20·7	1	0·0	0·7	0·0	21·5	8·8*	6·3*	1,490	3·4

Notes

(a) Details of the weight of tobacco consumed by products were obtained from *Estatistica Industrial* published by the National Institute of Statistics, Lisbon and from trade sources.

(b) The number of cigarettes consumed have been estimated from the cigarette consumption in pounds weight by using a conversion factor of 2·205 lbs. per 1,000. The conversion factor used for cigars and cigarillos was 12 lbs. per 1,000.

37. Sierra Leone

Year ended 30th September	Cigarettes		Cigars		Cigarillos		Smoking tobacco	Malawi leaf and shag†	Total	Population		Consumption per adult	
	Millions	Mn. lbs.	Millions	Mn. lbs.	Millions	Mn. lbs.	Mn. lbs.	Mn. lbs.	Mn. lbs.	Total Mns.	15+ Mns.	Cigarettes Number	Total Lbs.
1964	486	1·1	0	0·0	0	0·0	0·0	1·2	2·3	2·5*	1·8*	270	1·3
1965	512	1·1	1	0·0	0	0·0	0·0	1·5	2·7	2·5*	1·8*	280	1·5
1966	574	1·3	0	0·0	0	0·0	0·0	1·5	2·8	2·5*	1·9*	300	1·5
1967	467	1·0	0	0·0	0	0·0	0·0	1·6	2·7	2·8*	2·0*	230	1·4
1968	444	1·0	0	0·0	0	0·0	0·0	1·7	2·7	2·8*	2·0*	220	1·4
1969	498	1·1	0	0·0	0	0·0	0·0	1·9	3·0	2·8*	2·1*	240	1·4
1970	547	1·2	0	0·0	0	0·0	0·0	1·7	2·9	3·0*	2·4*	230	1·2
1971	707	1·6	0	0·0	0	0·0	0·0	1·0	2·6	3·0*	2·6*	270	1·0
1972	885	2·0	1	0·0	0	0·0	0·0	1·1	3·1	3·0*	2·6*	340	1·2
1973	1,115	2·5	1	0·0	0	0·0	0·0	1·0	3·5	3·0*	2·6*	430	1·3

† Malawi leaf and shag are used for hand-rolled cigarettes.

Notes

(a) Details of tobacco consumed by products were obtained from trade sources.

(b) Cigarette consumption in pounds weight has been estimated from the number of cigarettes consumed by using a conversion factor of 2·205 lbs. per 1,000. The conversion factors used for cigars and cigarillos were 7·36 lbs. per 1,000 and 2·75 lbs. per 1,000.

38. Singapore

Calendar year	Cigarettes		Cigars		Tobacco for hand-rolled cigarettes and pipe	Total Mn. lbs.	Population		Consumption per adult	
	Millions	Mn. lbs.	Millions	Mn. lbs.	Mn. lbs.		Total Mns.	15+ Mns.	Cigarettes Number	Total Lbs.
1964	2,565	6·4	2	0·0	0·1	6·5	1·8	1·1	2,330	5·9
1965	2,619	6·5	2	0·0	0·1	6·6	1·9	1·1	2,380	6·0
1966	2,737	6·8	2	0·0	0·1	6·9	1·9	1·1	2,490	6·2
1967	2,823	7·1	2	0·0	0·1	7·2	2·0	1·2	2,350	6·0
1968	2,758	6·9	2	0·0	0·0	6·9	2·0	1·2	2,300	5·8
1969	2,762	6·9	3	0·0	0·1	7·0	2·0	1·2	2,300	5·8
1970	2,828	7·1	3	0·0	0·1	7·2	2·1	1·3	2,180	5·5
1971	2,840	7·1	3	0·0	0·0	7·2	2·1	1·3	2,180	5·5
1972	2,983	7·5	3	0·0	0·0	7·6	2·1	1·3	2,290	5·8
1973	3,235	8·1	3	0·0	0·0	8·2	2·2	1·3	2,490	6·3

Notes

(a) Details of the numbers of cigarettes and cigars and of the weight of tobacco for hand-rolled cigarettes and pipe consumed were obtained from trade sources.

(b) Cigarette consumption in pounds weight has been estimated from the number of cigarettes consumed by using a conversion factor of 2·5 lbs. per 1,000. The conversion factor used for cigars was 3·7 lbs. per 1,000.

69

39. South Africa

Calendar year	Cigarettes		Cigars		Other manufactured tobacco	Snuff	Total	Population		Consumption per adult	
	Millions	Mn. lbs.	Millions	Mn. lbs.	Mn. lbs.	Mn. lbs.	Total Mn. lbs.	Total Mns.	15+ Mns.	Cigarettes Number	Total Lbs.
1920	1,517	3·3	16	0·2	10·1	0·1	13·7	6·8	4·0	380	3·4
1921	1,704	3·8	11	0·1	8·6	0·1	12·6	7·0	4·2*	410	3·0
1922	1,441	3·2	2	0·0	6·6	0·1	9·9	7·3	4·3*	340	2·3
1923	1,607	3·5	4	0·1	7·7	0·1	11·4	7·4*	4·4*	370	2·6
1924	1,669	3·7	4	0·1	8·2	0·1	12·1	7·5*	4·5*	370	2·7
1925	1,684	3·7	4	0·1	9·6	0·1	13·5	7·7	4·6*	370	2·9
1926	1,796	4·0	5	0·1	9·5	0·1	13·7	7·9*	4·7*	380	2·9
1927	2,244	4·9	7	0·1	11·0	0·1	16·1	8·0*	4·8*	470	3·4
1928	2,372	5·2	7	0·1	10·7	0·1	16·1	8·2*	4·9*	480	3·3
1929	2,417	5·3	4	0·1	10·1	0·1	15·6	8·3*	5·0*	480	3·1
1930	2,651	5·8	5	0·1	10·9	0·1	16·9	8·5	5·1*	520	3·3
1931	...	...	...	...	...	...	...	...	...	...	...
1932	...	...	...	...	...	...	...	...	...	...	...
1933	2,277	5·0	5	0·1	10·5	0·1	15·7	9·1	5·5*	410	2·9
1934	2,608	5·8	6	0·1	11·3	0·1	17·3	9·3	5·7*	460	3·0
1935	2,951	6·5	6	0·1	11·5	0·1	18·2	9·4	5·7*	520	3·2
1936	3,337	7·1	7	0·1	12·1	0·1	19·4	9·6	5·9	570	3·3
1937	3,755	9·1	7	0·1	12·6	0·1	21·9	9·8	6·0*	630	3·7
1938	4,075	9·8	7	0·1	13·8	0·2	23·9	10·0	6·1*	670	3·9
1939	4,204	10·2	7	0·1	14·3	0·2	24·8	10·2	6·3*	670	3·9
1940	4,625	10·9	8	0·1	14·5	0·3	25·8	10·4	6·4*	720	4·0
1941	5,268	12·3	10	0·1	16·4	0·3	29·1	10·6	6·6*	800	4·4
1942	6,397	14·7	9	0·1	16·2	0·1	31·1	10·9	6·8*	940	4·6
1943	7,293	16·9	10	0·1	13·9	0·2	31·1	11·0	6·8*	1,070	4·6
1944	7,266	16·8	10	0·1	14·1	0·2	31·2	11·1	6·9*	1,050	4·5
1945	7,621	17·7	11	0·1	14·2	0·2	32·2	11·3	7·1	1,070	4·5
1946	8,064	18·1	8	0·1	15·6	0·2	34·0	11·4	7·1*	1,140	4·8
1947	8,050	18·0	5	0·1	15·0	0·1	33·2	11·7	7·3*	1,100	4·5
1948	8,747	19·1	4	0·1	16·7	0·2	36·1	12·0	7·5*	1,170	4·8
1949	9,411	20·0	...	0·1*	17·2	0·2	37·5*	12·2	7·6*	1,240	4·9

South Africa (contd)

Calendar year	Cigarettes Millions	Cigarettes Mn. lbs.	Cigars Millions	Cigars Mn. lbs.	Other manufactured tobacco Mn. lbs.	Snuff Mn. lbs.	Total Mn. lbs.	Population Total Mns.	Population 15+ Mns.	Consumption per adult Cigarettes Number	Consumption per adult Total Lbs.
1950	9,089	19·3	7	0·1	18·7	0·2	38·3	12·5	7·8*	1,170	4·9
1951	9,545	20·8	6	0·1	19·4	0·5	40·8	12·7	7·9	1,210	5·2
1952	9,889	21·4	3	0·0	20·0	0·6	42·0	12·9	8·0*	1,240	5·3
1953	9,969	21·7	4	0·0	20·7	0·2	42·6	13·2	8·2*	1,220	5·2
1954	10,107	22·4	3	0·0	21·9	0·2	44·5	13·4	8·3*	1,220	5·4
1955	10,548	25·2	3	0·0	21·2	0·0	46·4	14·5	9·0	1,170	5·2
1956	10,824	24·9	3	0·0	22·7	0·0	47·6	14·7	9·1	1,190	5·2
1957	11,364	26·5	2	0·0	23·1	0·0	49·6	15·0	9·3	1,220	5·3
1958	11,028	25·9	2	0·0	21·1	0·0	47·0	15·2	9·4	1,170	5·0
1959	10,332	24·4	2	0·0	21·7	0·0	46·1	15·6	9·7	1,070	4·8
1960	10,620	25·2	2	0·0	21·9	0·0	47·1	15·8	9·8	1,080	4·8
1961	10,392	24·3	2	0·0	21·4	0·0	45·7	16·1	10·0	1,040	4·6
1962	10,690	24·3	2	0·0	21·9	0·0	46·2	16·6	10·4	1,030	4·4
1963	11,554	26·2	38	0·2	23·2	0·2	49·8	17·0	11·5	1,000	4·3
1964	12,212	27·8	46	0·3	23·6	0·2	51·9	17·5	11·8	1,030	4·4
1965	13,080	29·3	55	0·3	25·6	0·2	55·4	17·9	12·1	1,080	4·6
1966	14,088	30·3	54	0·3	24·7	0·2	55·5	18·3	12·4	1,140	4·5
1967	13,934	30·3	48	0·3	24·2	0·2	55·0	18·7	11·6	1,200	4·7
1968	15,427	33·4	53	0·3	26·5	0·2	60·4	19·4	12·0	1,290	5·0
1969	16,619	35·7	77	0·5	25·8	0·2	62·2	20·2	12·5	1,330	5·0
1970	18,029	38·4	98	0·6	26·7	0·2	65·9	21·4	13·3	1,360	5·0
1971	18,088	39·8	133	1·2	25·7	0·2	66·9	22·1	13·4	1,350	5·0
1972	18,515	40·7	215	2·0	26·1	0·2	69·0	22·7	13·7	1,350	5·0
1973	19,717	43·4	263	2·5	27·1	0·2	73·2	23·4	14·3	1,380	5·1

Notes
(a) Details of the consumption of cigarettes and cigars and of other tobacco products in South Africa were obtained from the South Africa Tobacco Industry Control Board, the Bureau of Census and Statistics and the Customs and Excise.
(b) For the period 1920–1954 a conversion factor of 2·205 lbs. per 1,000 was used to estimate the cigarette consumption in pounds weight from the number of cigarettes consumed. From 1955 onwards the Customs and Excise Department provided details of the numbers of cigarettes consumed and the weight of tobacco used for the manufacture of cigarettes. The conversion factor used for cigars was 11·5 lbs. per 1,000 for the years up to 1951. For the period 1963 to 1973 a conversion factor of 9 lbs. per 1,000 was used, except in the case of Dutch cigars where actual numbers and weights were available.

40. Spain

Calendar year	Cigarettes		Cigars		Smoking tobacco	Total	Population		Consumption per adult	
	Millions	Mn. lbs.	Millions	Mn. lbs.	Mn. lbs.	Mn. lbs.	Total Mns.	15 + Mns.	Cigarettes Number	Total Lbs.
1927	5,416	11·9	315	4·7	42·4	59·0	22·7*	15·5*	350	3·8
1928	6,592	14·5	287	4·3	42·0	60·8	22·9*	15·7*	420	3·9
1929	7,367	16·2	275	4·1	40·0	60·3	23·1*	15·9*	460	3·8
1930	7,822	17·2	266	4·0	39·6	60·8	23·4	16·2*	480	3·8
1931	7,611	16·8	272	4·1	40·4	61·3	23·7*	16·4*	460	3·7
1932	8,198	18·1	284	4·3	38·9	61·3	23·9	16·5*	500	3·7
1933	7,775	17·1	285	4·3	35·2	56·6	24·1	16·7*	470	3·4
1934	7,117	15·7	268	4·0	38·8	58·5	24·3	16·9*	420	3·5
1935	6,718	14·8	250	3·8	41·8	60·4	24·6	17·1*	390	3·5
1940	6,756	14·9	110	1·6	26·1	42·6	25·8	18·0	380	2·4
1941	7,198	15·9	98	1·5	16·0	33·4	26·0	18·2*	400	1·8
1942	7,440	16·4	93	1·4	12·9	30·7	26·2	18·3*	410	1·7
1943	9,160	20·2	69	1·0	14·3	35·5	26·4	18·5*	500	1·9
1944	8,813	19·4	73	1·1	21·1	41·6	26·6	18·6*	470	2·2
1945	9,192	20·3	69	1·0	30·4	51·1	26·8	18·8	490	2·8
1946	10,261	22·6	68	1·0	40·1	63·7	27·0	18·9*	540	3·4
1947	10,927	24·1	62	0·9	33·9	58·9	27·2	19·1*	570	3·1
1948	9,783	21·6	63	0·9	32·4	54·9	27·4	19·2	510	2·9
1949	10,010	22·1	61	0·9	41·4	64·4	27·7	19·9*	500	3·2
1950	8,825	19·5	80	1·2	42·7	63·4	27·9	20·6	430	3·1
1951	9,682	21·3	89	1·3	35·9	58·5	28·1	20·7*	470	2·8
1952	11,538	25·4	89	1·3	45·4	72·1	28·3	20·9*	550	3·4
1953	12,707	28·0	88	1·3	27·5	56·8	28·5	21·0*	610	2·7
1954	13,839	30·5	90	1·4	33·0	64·9	28·8	21·3*	650	3·0

Spain (contd)

Calendar year	Cigarettes		Cigars		Smoking tobacco	Total	Population		Consumption per adult	
	Millions	Mn. lbs.	Millions	Mn. lbs.	Mn. lbs.	Total Mn. lbs.	Total Mns.	15 + Mns.	Cigarettes Number	Total Lbs.
1955	15,554	34·3	98	1·5	31·8	67·6	29·0	21·4*	730	3·2
1956	15,109	33·3	144	2·1	28·7	64·1	29·2	21·5*	700	3·0
1957	18,222	40·2	175	2·6	26·3	69·1	29·4	21·7*	840	3·2
1958	21,872	48·2	193	2·9	26·5	77·6	29·7	21·9*	1,000	3·5
1959	22,839	50·3	193	2·9	22·5	75·7	30·0	22·1*	1,030	3·4
1960	24,892	54·9	180	2·7	20·3	77·9	30·1	22·2	1,120	3·5
1961	27,220	60·1	199	3·0	18·8	81·9	30·6	22·3*	1,220	3·7
1962	30,294	66·8	210	3·2	15·4	85·4	30·8	22·4*	1,350	3·8
1963	33,915	74·8	276	4·1	11·6	90·5	31·1	22·5*	1,510	4·0
1964	36,570	80·6	337	5·1	9·3	95·0	31·3	22·6*	1,620	4·2
1965	40,087	88·4	397	6·0	9·0	103·4	31·6	22·8*	1,760	4·5
1966	42,324	93·3	461	6·9	7·9	108·1	31·9	23·0*	1,840	4·7
1967	44,999	99·2	493	7·4	6·5	113·1	32·3	23·2*	1,940	4·9
1968	47,174	104·0	515	7·7	5·6	117·3	32·6	23·4*	2,020	5·0
1969	47,287	104·3	502	7·5	5·1	116·9	32·9	23·7*	2,000	4·9
1970	50,084	110·4	560	8·4	4·3	123·1	33·3	24·0*	2,090	5·1
1971	50,843	112·1	606	9·1	3·9	125·1	34·0	24·5*	2,080	5·1
1972	53,234	117·4	671	10·1	3·5	131·0	34·5	24·8*	2,150	5·3
1973	56,623	124·9	763	11·4	3·3	139·6	34·7	25·0*	2,260	5·6

Notes

(a) For the years 1927–1955 details of the weight of cigarettes, cigars and smoking tobacco consumed were obtained from *Annuario Estadistico de Espana*, 1957. Figures for the years 1956–1973 were provided by the National Institute of Statistics, Madrid.

(b) The number of cigarettes consumed have been estimated from the cigarette consumption in pounds weight by using a conversion factor of 2·205 lbs. per 1,000. The conversion factor used for cigars was 15 lbs. per 1,000.

73

41. Sweden

Calendar year	Cigarettes		Cigars		Cigarillos		Smoking tobacco	Chewing tobacco	Snuff	Total	Population		Consumption per adult	
	Millions	Mn. lbs.	Millions	Mn. lbs.	Millions	Mn. lbs.	Mn. lbs.	Mn. lbs.	Mn. lbs.	Total Mn. lbs.	Total Mns.	15+ Mns.	Cigarettes Number	Total Lbs.
1920	1,559	1·8	89	1·2	118	0·7	1·7	0·8	14·4	20·6	5·9	4·2	370	4·9
1921	1,345	1·6	58	0·8	117	0·7	1·8	0·7	13·4	19·0	5·9*	4·2*	320	4·5
1922	1,123	1·4	62	0·8	118	0·7	2·0	0·6	12·5	18·0	5·9*	4·2*	270	4·3
1923	1,058	1·3	40	0·5	120	0·8	2·1	0·6	12·1	17·4	6·0*	4·3*	250	4·0
1924	1,089	1·4	39	0·5	128	0·8	2·2	0·5	11·8	17·2	6·0*	4·3*	250	4·0
1925	1,085	1·4	39	0·6	137	0·9	2·3	0·5	11·7	17·4	6·0	4·4*	250	4·0
1926	1,204	1·5	41	0·6	141	0·9	2·3	0·5	11·6	17·4	6·1*	4·5*	270	3·9
1927	1,284	1·6	40	0·6	141	0·9	2·2	0·4	11·3	17·0	6·1*	4·5*	290	3·8
1928	1,446	1·9	39	0·6	146	0·9	2·2	0·4	11·0	17·0	6·1*	4·5*	320	3·8
1929	1,640	2·1	37	0·6	160	1·0	2·2	0·4	10·7	17·0	6·1*	4·6*	360	3·7
1930	1,864	2·4	36	0·5	174	1·1	2·1	0·3	10·7	17·1	6·1	4·6	410	3·7
1931	1,999	2·8	32	0·5	171	1·1	2·0	0·3	10·7	17·4	6·2*	4·7*	430	3·7
1932	2,012	3·0	31	0·4	171	1·1	2·2	0·3	10·7	17·7	6·2	4·7*	430	3·8
1933	1,894	2·9	29	0·4	170	1·0	2·2	0·3	10·5	17·3	6·2	4·8*	390	3·6
1934	1,878	3·3	29	0·4	174	1·0	2·2	0·2	10·1	17·2	6·2	4·8*	390	3·6
1935	1,843	3·6	27	0·4	179	1·1	2·2	0·2	9·9	17·4	6·2	4·9	380	3·6
1936	1,806	3·9	26	0·4	187	1·1	2·3	0·2	9·7	17·6	6·3	4·9*	370	3·6
1937	1,822	4·2	26	0·4	193	1·1	2·3	0·2	9·7	17·9	6·3	4·9	370	3·7
1938	1,889	4·5	25	0·3	196	1·2	2·4	0·2	9·6	18·2	6·3	5·0	380	3·6
1939	1,976	4·8	23	0·3	197	1·2	2·4	0·2	9·4	18·3	6·3	5·0*	400	3·7
1940	2,126	5·3	20	0·3	176	1·0	3·0	0·2	8·6	18·4	6·4	5·1	420	3·6
1941	2,191	5·1	25	0·3	204	1·0	3·4	0·2	8·5	18·5	6·4	5·1	430	3·6
1942	2,235	3·3	24	0·3	171	0·9	3·7	0·1	7·5	15·8	6·4	5·1*	440	3·1
1943	2,237	3·7	34	0·4	158	0·8	3·7	0·1	7·2	15·9	6·5	5·1*	440	3·1
1944	2,307	5·2	30	0·4	160	0·9	4·4	0·1	7·7	18·7	6·6	5·2*	440	3·6
1945	2,468	6·2	28	0·4	154	0·9	4·3	0·1	7·7	19·6	6·6	5·2	470	3·8
1946	3,141	8·2	30	0·4	157	0·9	3·8	0·1	7·7	21·1	6·7	5·2	600	4·1
1947	3,670	9·5	27	0·4	146	0·8	3·4	0·1	7·6	21·8	6·8	5·3	690	4·1
1948	3,809	9·9	26	0·3	144	0·8	3·6	0·1	7·4	22·1	6·9	5·3	720	4·2
1949	3,984	10·3	23	0·3	134	0·7	3·4	0·1	7·1	21·9	7·0	5·4	740	4·1

Sweden (contd)

Calendar year	Cigarettes		Cigars		Cigarillos		Smoking tobacco	Chewing tobacco	Snuff	Total	Population		Consumption per adult	
	Millions	Mn. lbs.	Millions	Mn. lbs.	Millions	Mn. lbs.	Mn. lbs.	Mn. lbs.	Mn. lbs.	Total Mn. lbs.	Total Mns.	15+ Mns.	Cigarettes Number	Total Lbs.
1950	4,352	10·7	23	0·3	133	0·7	3·3	0·1	6·9	22·0	7·0	5·4	810	4·1
1951	4,416	10·7	20	0·3	104	0·5	3·1	0·1	6·4	21·1	7·1	5·4	820	3·9
1952	5,121	12·2	21	0·3	114	0·6	3·3	0·1	6·5	23·0	7·1	5·4	950	4·3
1953	5,248	12·3	20	0·3	115	0·6	3·3	0·1	6·4	23·0	7·2	5·5	950	4·2
1954	5,289	12·2	23	0·3	129	0·6	3·3	0·1	6·4	22·9	7·2	5·5	960	4·2
1955	5,548	12·7	23	0·3	135	0·6	3·2	0·1	6·3	23·2	7·3	5·5	1,010	4·2
1956	5,714	13·1	21	0·3	130	0·6	3·0	0·1	6·1	23·2	7·3	5·6	1,020	4·1
1957	5,903	13·4	21	0·3	134	0·6	2·9	0·1	6·0	23·3	7·4	5·6*	1,050	4·2
1958	6,066	13·7	20	0·2	137	0·6	3·2	0·1	5·9	23·7	7·4	5·7	1,060	4·2
1959	6,240	14·4	19	0·2	142	0·6	3·3	0·1	5·8	24·4	7·4	5·7	1,090	4·3
1960	6,740	15·6	21	0·3	197	0·8	3·5	0·1	5·9	26·2	7·5	5·8	1,160	4·5
1961	7,216	16·6	19	0·2	188	0·8	3·4	0·1	5·7	26·8	7·5	5·9	1,220	4·5
1962	7,498	17·1	19	0·2	195	0·8	3·4	0·1	5·6	27·2	7·6	5·9	1,270	4·6
1963	7,860	17·6	223	1·0	Combined with cigars		3·4	0·0	5·6	27·6	7·6	6·0	1,310	4·6
1964	7,810	17·5	310	1·4	Combined with cigars		3·8	0·0	5·6	28·3	7·7	6·1	1,280	4·6
1965	8,300	18·0	311	1·3	Combined with cigars		3·8	0·0	5·5	28·6	7·7	6·1	1,360	4·7
1966	8,700	19·0	318	1·3	Combined with cigars		3·8	0·0	5·5	29·6	7·8	6·2	1,400	4·8
1967	8,927	18·4	331	1·5	Combined with cigars		3·8	0·0	5·3	29·0	7·9	6·2	1,440	4·7
1968	9,679	19·0	333	1·5	Combined with cigars		3·7	0·0	5·2	29·4	7·9	6·3	1,550	4·7
1969	10,147	19·1	334	1·4	Combined with cigars		3·5	0·0	5·3	29·3	8·0	6·3	1,610	4·6
1970	10,269	18·4	326	1·4	Combined with cigars		3·5	0·0	5·5	28·8	8·0	6·4	1,620	4·5
1971	9,957	17·1	282	1·2	Combined with cigars		3·4	0·0	5·8	27·5	8·1	6·4	1,550	4·3
1972	11,243	19·2	254	1·1	Combined with cigars		3·1	0·0	5·9	29·3	8·1	6·4	1,610	4·6
1973	9,265	15·6	249	1·0	Combined with cigars		3·2	0·0	6·0	25·8	8·1	6·5	1,580	4·0

Notes

(a) Details of the number and weight of cigarettes, cigars and cigarillos and of the weight of smoking tobacco, chewing tobacco and snuff consumed were obtained from the Annual Reports of the Swedish Tobacco Monopoly (now the Swedish Tobacco Company).

(b) Figures for cigarette consumption per adult in 1972 and 1973 have been corrected for the effect of hoarding prior to an increase in cigarette tax on 1st January, 1973.

42. Switzerland

Calendar year	Cigarettes Millions	Cigarettes Mn. lbs.	Cigars Millions	Cigars Mn. lbs.	Smoking tobacco Mn. lbs.	Total Mn. lbs.	Population Total Mns.	Population 15+ Mns.	Consumption per adult Cigarettes Number	Consumption per adult Total Lbs.
1934	1,728	3·8	481	5·3	5·8	14·9	4·2	3·2*	540	4·7
1935										
1936										
1937										
1938										
1939	2,262	5·0	500	5·5	5·6	16·1	4·2	3·3	690	4·9
1940	2,746	6·0	611	6·7	6·1	18·8	4·3	3·3	830	5·7
1941	2,715	6·0	573	6·3	6·1	18·4	4·3	3·3	820	5·6
1942	3,167	7·0	567	6·3	5·7	19·0	4·3	3·4	930	5·6
1943	3,444	7·6	499	5·5	5·1	18·2	4·4	3·4	1,010	5·4
1944										
1945	3,964	8·7	473	5·2	4·6	18·5	4·4	3·4	1,170	5·4
1946	4,416	9·7	569	6·3	6·5	22·5	4·5	3·5	1,260	6·4
1947	5,009	11·0	597	6·6	5·5	23·1	4·5	3·5	1,430	6·6
1948	4,989	11·0	559	6·2	4·8	22·0	4·6	3·5	1,430	6·3
1949	5,143	11·3	437	4·8	4·7	20·8	4·6	3·6	1,430	5·8
1950	5,405	11·9	440	4·9	4·9	21·7	4·7	3·6	1,500	6·0
1951	5,672	11·9	470	5·2	4·9	22·0	4·7	3·6	1,580	6·1
1952	6,222	13·7	477	5·3	4·7	23·7	4·8	3·6	1,730	6·6
1953	6,191	13·0	489	5·4	4·7	23·1	4·9	3·7	1,670	6·2
1954	6,236	13·1	478	5·3	4·5	22·9	4·9	3·7	1,690	6·2
1955	6,625	13·9	504	5·6	4·4	23·9	5·0	3·8	1,740	6·3
1956	7,081	14·9	477	5·3	4·3	24·5	5·0	3·8	1,860	6·4
1957	7,488	15·0	454	5·0	4·1	24·1	5·1	3·9	1,920	6·2
1958	8,248	16·5	502	5·5	4·1	26·1	5·2	3·9	2,110	6·7
1959	8,557	17·1	492	5·4	4·1	26·6	5·2	4·0	2,140	6·7

Switzerland (contd)

Calendar year	Cigarettes		Cigars		Smoking tobacco	Total	Population		Consumption per adult	
	Millions	Mn. lbs.	Millions	Mn. lbs.	Mn. lbs.	Mn. lbs.	Total Mns.	15+ Mns.	Cigarettes Number	Total Lbs.
1960	9,751	19·5	478	5·2	3·7	28·5	5·4	4·1	2,380	7·0
1961	10,866	21·7	517	5·7	3·8	31·2	5·5	4·2	2,590	7·4
1962	11,691	23·4	588	6·5	3·7	33·6	5·6	4·2	2,780	8·0
1963	11,986	26·4	582	6·4	3·8	36·6	5·8	4·4	2,720	8·3
1964	11,550	25·5	639	7·0	3·6	36·1	5·9	4·5	2,570	8·0
1965	13,728	30·3	620	6·8	3·5	40·6	5·9	4·5	3,050	9·0
1966	11,051	24·4	624	6·9	3·0	34·3	6·0	4·6	2,400	7·5
1967	12,715	28·0	634	7·0	3·1	38·1	6·0	4·6	2,760	8·3
1968	13,603	30·0	661	7·3	2·9	40·2	6·0	4·6	2,960	8·7
1969	15,427	34·0	650	7·2	2·8	44·0	6·1	4·7	3,280	9·4
1970	16,300	35·9	662	7·3	2·7	45·9	6·2	4·7	3,470	9·8
1971	17,900	39·4	679	7·4	2·2	49·0	6·2	4·7	3,810	10·4
1972	18,700	41·2	744	8·1	2·2	51·5	6·3	4·8	3,900	10·7
1973	16,500	36·3	727	7·9	2·0	46·2	6·4	4·9	3,370	9·4

Notes
(a) Details of the production, import and export of the numbers of cigarettes and cigars and of the weight of pipe tobacco from which consumption data was calculated were provided by the Federal Bureau of Statistics, Berne and the Swiss Customs Administration. Statistics of sales of tobacco goods in Switzerland were provided by the Swiss Cigarette Manufacturers Association.
(b) Factors for converting the numbers of cigarettes and numbers of cigars consumed into pounds weight were provided by trade sources in Switzerland.
(c) Details of the amount of tobacco consumed in individual years before 1941 were not provided. The figures shown above for the years 1934 to 1940 are annual averages.
(d) The consumption per adult figures shown in this table are exaggerated due to the increasing consumption by borderers, tourists and seasonal workers. It is estimated that these three categories represented 30% to 35% of Swiss sales in recent years.
(e) The source of the population figures was the *Annuaire Statistique de la Suisse*.

43. Turkey

Calendar year	Cigarettes		Smoking tobacco	Cigars, snuff and tombac†	Total	Population		Consumption per adult	
	Millions	Mn. lbs.	Mn. lbs.	Mn. lbs.	Total Mn. lbs.	Total Mns.	15+ Mns.	Cigarettes Number	Total Lbs.
1925	1,941	4·3	8·4	0·0	12·7	13·0*	7·4*	260	1·7
1926	3,373	7·4	13·0	0·2	20·6	13·3*	7·6*	440	2·7
1927	4,644	10·2	11·0	0·3	21·5	13·6	7·8*	600	2·7
1928	5,925	13·1	8·8	0·3	22·2	13·9*	8·0*	740	2·8
1929	7,111	15·7	7·2	0·3	23·2	14·2*	8·2*	870	2·8
1930	7,134	15·7	6·0	0·2	21·9	14·5	8·4*	850	2·6
1931	6,362	14·0	5·1	0·2	19·3	14·8*	8·6*	740	2·2
1932	8,428	18·6	4·6	0·2	23·4	15·1*	8·8*	960	2·7
1933	8,867	19·6	5·1	0·2	24·9	15·4*	9·0*	990	2·8
1934	8,459	18·7	5·1	0·2	24·0	15·8*	9·2*	920	2·6
1935	9,077	20·0	5·9	0·2	26·1	16·2	9·5	960	2·7
1936	9,123	20·1	6·7	0·2	27·0	16·5*	9·7*	940	2·8
1937	9,325	20·6	7·4	0·2	28·2	16·8	9·9*	940	2·8
1938	9,813	21·6	8·1	0·2	29·9	17·0	10·1*	970	3·0
1939	10,058	22·2	9·3	0·2	31·7	17·5	10·4*	970	3·0
1940	10,072	22·2	10·4	0·2	32·8	17·8	10·6*	950	3·1
1941	11,843	26·1	9·7	0·2	36·0	18·0	10·8*	1,100	3·3
1942	12,622	27·8	9·1	0·1	37·0	18·2	10·9*	1,160	3·4
1943	13,687	30·2	8·5	0·0	38·7	18·4	11·1*	1,230	3·5
1944	15,024	33·1	6·7	0·1	39·9	18·6	11·2*	1,340	3·6
1945	15,723	34·7	6·1	0·1	40·9	18·8	11·4	1,380	3·6
1946	14,672	32·4	6·0	0·1	38·5	19·2	11·7*	1,250	3·3
1947	15,281	33·7	5·7	0·1	39·5	19·6	11·9*	1,280	3·3
1948	15,001	33·1	6·1	0·1	39·3	20·0	12·2*	1,230	3·2
1949	15,183	33·5	5·8	0·1	39·4	20·5	12·6*	1,210	3·1

† Tombac is the tobacco used in water-pipes.

Turkey (contd)

Calendar year	Cigarettes Millions	Cigarettes Mn. lbs.	Smoking tobacco Mn. lbs.	Cigars, snuff and tombac† Mn. lbs.	Total Mn. lbs.	Population Total Mns.	15+ Mns.	Consumption per adult Cigarettes Number	Consumption per adult Total Lbs.
1950	15,762	34·8	5·5	0·1	40·4	20·9	12·9	1,220	3·1
1951	17,002	37·5	5·7	0·1	43·3	21·5	13·2*	1,290	3·3
1952	18,673	41·2	6·3	0·1	47·6	22·2	13·5*	1,380	3·5
1953	20,428	45·0	6·0	0·2	51·2	22·8	13·8*	1,480	3·7
1954	22,606	49·8	6·0	0·2	56·0	23·4	14·2*	1,590	3·9
1955	22,461	49·5	6·1	0·2	55·8	24·1	14·5	1,550	3·8
1956	23,401	51·6	6·5	0·2	58·3	24·8	14·8*	1,580	3·9
1957	25,996	57·3	6·8	0·2	64·3	25·5*	15·2*	1,710	4·2
1958	27,933	61·6	4·5	0·3	66·4	26·2	15·5	1,800	4·3
1959	26,702	58·9	6·4	0·2	65·5	27·0	15·8	1,690	4·1
1960	27,171	59·9	6·8	0·2	66·9	27·8	16·1	1,690	4·2
1961	28,320	62·4	7·9	0·2	70·5	28·6	16·4	1,730	4·3
1962	29,689	65·4	8·8	0·3	74·5	29·4	16·8	1,770	4·4
1963	29,407	64·8	9·5	0·2	74·5	29·9	16·7	1,760	4·5
1964	30,471	67·2	7·9	0·2	75·3	30·6	17·1	1,780	4·4
1965	31,867	70·3	7·1	0·2	77·6	31·4	17·5	1,820	4·4
1966	34,195	75·4	7·2	0·3	82·9	32·3	18·0	1,900	4·6
1967	34,166	75·3	7·0	0·3	82·6	33·0	19·1	1,800	4·3
1968	35,974	79·3	6·3	0·3	85·9	33·9	19·6	1,830	4·4
1969	36,644	80·8	6·6	0·3	87·7	34·7	20·1	1,820	4·4
1970	39,552	87·2	6·7	0·3	94·2	35·7	20·7	1,910	4·6
1971	41,607	91·7	6·7	0·3	98·7	36·6	21·2	1,960	4·7
1972	44,319	97·7	6·6	0·3	104·6	37·4	21·6	2,050	4·8

† Tombac is the tobacco used in water-pipes.

Notes
(a) Details of the weight of tobacco consumed by types of product were provided by the Turkish State Monopolies, Istanbul.
(b) The numbers of cigarettes consumed have been estimated from the cigarette consumption in pounds weight by using a conversion factor of 2·205 lbs. per 1,000.

44. United Kingdom

Calendar year	Cigarettes Millions	Cigarettes Mn. lbs.	Cigars Millions	Snuff Mn. lbs.	Snuff Mn. lbs.	Tobacco for hand-rolled cigarettes and pipe Mn. lbs.	Total Mn. lbs.	Population Total Mns.	Population 15+ Mns.	Consumption per adult Cigarettes Number	Consumption per adult Total Lbs.
1920	36,240	80·3	...	2·6		70·3	153·2	46·5	33·5	1,080	4·6
1921	35,185	78·1	...	2·6		69·0	149·7	47·1	34·2	1,030	4·4
1922	33,730	75·0	...	2·6		67·1	144·7	47·4	34·5	980	4·2
1923	33,725	75·1	...	2·6		63·1	140·8	44·6	32·7	1,030	4·3
1924	33,835	75·1	...	2·7		58·0	135·8	44·9	33·0	1,030	4·1
1925	36,030	80·1	...	2·6		58·1	140·8	45·1	33·3	1,080	4·2
1926	37,435	83·1	...	2·6		56·1	141·8	45·2	33·6	1,110	4·2
1927	40,030	89·1	...	2·6		55·1	146·8	45·4	33·8	1,180	4·3
1928	43,035	95·5	135	1·0	1·4	54·8	152·7	45·6	34·1	1,260	4·5
1929	45,535	101·3	135	1·0	1·4	53·3	157·0	45·7	34·3	1,330	4·6
1930	48,335	107·0	140	0·9	1·4	51·5	160·8	45·9	35·1	1,380	4·6
1931	49,235	108·7	150	0·9	1·3	49·8	160·7	46·1	34·9	1,410	4·6
1932	49,630	109·3	135	0·9	1·1	47·2	158·5	46·3	35·2	1,410	4·5
1933	52,130	114·6	135	0·9	1·1	45·6	162·2	46·5	35·5	1,470	4·6
1934	53,625	118·9	145	0·9	1·2	45·9	166·9	46·7	35·8	1,500	4·7
1935	57,330	126·8	155	1·0	1·3	45·0	174·1	46·9	36·1	1,590	4·8
1936	61,635	136·8	165	1·0	1·3	44·2	183·3	47·1	36·4	1,690	5·0
1937	65,835	147·0	170	1·0	1·4	43·2	192·6	47·3	36·8	1,790	5·2
1938	69,740	155·8	170	1·0	1·3	43·0	201·1	47·5	37·1	1,880	5·4
1939	73,810	162·8	175	1·0	1·1	41·6	206·5	47·8	37·5	1,970	5·5
1940	74,805	161·1	125	1·0	0·8	40·2	203·1	47·2	37·1	2,020	5·5
1941	82,760	179·3	155	1·1	0·9	42·9	224·2	47·2	37·1	2,230	6·0
1942	86,110	188·3	150	1·2	1·0	43·9	234·4	46·9	36·8	2,340	6·4
1943	85,475	189·3	155	1·1	1·0	38·8	230·2	46·8	36·7	2,330	6·3
1944	84,525	189·8	130	1·2	0·9	37·4	229·3	45·8	35·6	2,370	6·4
1945	93,300	209·0	120	1·1	0·9	38·4	249·4	46·2	35·9	2,600	6·9
1946	99,015	222·0	100	1·0	0·8	41·7	265·5	48·4	38·1	2,600	7·0
1947	87,525	193·2	125	0·8	1·2	37·6	232·8	49·2	38·5	2,270	6·0
1948	84,180	184·0	110	0·8	0·9	41·0	226·7	49·7	38·8	2,170	5·8
1949	81,950	177·9	105	0·7	0·8	40·9	220·3	50·0	38·9	2,110	5·7

United Kingdom (contd)

Calendar year	Cigarettes Millions	Cigarettes Mn. lbs.	Cigars and cigarillos Millions	Mn. lbs.	Cigarillos† Millions	Mn. lbs.	Snuff Mn. lbs.	Tobacco for hand-rolled cigarettes and pipe Mn. lbs.	Total Mn. lbs.	Population Total Mns.	15+ Mns.	Cigarettes Number	Total Lbs.
1950	85,145	181·7	115	0·8			0·7	38·3	221·5	50·3	39·1	2,180	5·7
1951	89,335	190·8	120	0·8			0·7	35·9	228·2	50·2	38·9	2,300	5·9
1952	90,400	194·0	125	0·9			0·7	36·7	232·3	50·4	39·0	2,320	6·0
1953	92,695	198·6	130	0·8			0·8	35·8	236·0	50·6	39·1	2,370	6·0
1954	95,230	204·0	140	0·9			0·7	35·3	240·9	50·8	39·2	2,430	6·1
1955	98,670	211·1	150	0·9			0·7	33·8	246·5	51·0	39·3	2,510	6·3
1956	99,560	215·5	180	1·0			0·7	32·3	249·5	51·2	39·4	2,530	6·3
1957	102,250	221·3	210	1·2			0·7	32·8	256·0	51·5	39·5	2,590	6·5
1958	104,020	225·1	250	1·3			0·7	33·6	260·7	51·7	39·6	2,630	6·6
1959	106,600	230·3	290	1·5			0·6	33·7	266·1	52·0	39·9	2,670	6·7
1960	110,900	239·2	315	1·6			0·6	33·2	274·6	52·4	40·2	2,760	6·8
1961	113,400	243·1	315	1·6			0·6	32·4	277·7	52·8	40·4	2,810	6·9
1962	109,900	230·9	390	1·9			0·6	33·0	266·4	53·3	41·0*	2,680	6·5
1963	115,200	237·8	445	2·1			0·5	32·8	273·2	53·6	41·3*	2,790	6·6
1964	114,400	230·8	590	2·7			0·5	32·5	266·5	53·9	41·6*	2,750	6·4
1965	112,000	220·7	700	2·9			0·5	30·7	254·8	54·2	41·8*	2,680	6·1
1966	117,600	223·3	900	3·5			0·5	29·7	257·0	54·5	41·9*	2,810	6·1
1967	119,100	221·3	1,135	4·0			0·5	29·6	255·4	54·8	41·9*	2,840	6·1
			Cigars Millions	Mn. lbs.	Cigarillos† Millions	Mn. lbs.							
1968	121,800	220·2	835	3·5	345	0·5	0·5	28·6	253·4	55·0	42·0*	2,900	6·0
1969	124,900	216·5	845	3·6	290	0·5	0·5	28·2	249·3	55·3	42·0*	2,970	5·9
1970	127,900	215·4	975	4·1	215	0·4	0·4	27·1	247·4	55·4	42·0*	3,050	5·9
1971	122,400	204·1	1,360	5·7	195	0·3	0·4	26·3	236·8	55·6	42·1*	2,910	5·6
1972	130,500	216·2	1,410	6·1	165	0·3	0·4	26·1	249·1	55·8	42·3*	3,090	5·9
1973	137,400	228·9	1,545	6·9	170	0·3	0·4	25·8	262·3	55·9	42·6*	3,230	6·2
1974	137,000	225·6	1,600	6·8	165	0·3	0·4	25·4	258·5	56·0	42·7*	3,210	6·1

† Cigarillos are products manufactured from cigar tobacco and are of approximately cigarette size, wrapped in either paper or processed tobacco sheet of natural tobacco colour.

Notes

(a) The weight of manufactured cigarettes, cigars, snuff and other tobaccos sold to the public have been estimated from trade sources.

(b) The conversion factors for cigarettes and cigars have been estimated by the trade and include allowances for changes in the ratio of large to small cigarettes and for the growth of filter cigarettes.

(c) Population figures were obtained from the *Registrar General's Statistical Reviews* and the *Monthly Digest of Statistics*, published by H.M. Stationery Office.

(d) More detailed information of the consumption of tobacco goods in the United Kingdom may be found in *Statistics of Smoking in the United Kingdom*, Research Paper No. 1 published by the Tobacco Research Council.

45. U.S.A.

Calendar year	Cigarettes Millions	Cigarettes Mn. lbs.	Cigars Millions	Cigars Mn. lbs.	Tobacco for hand-rolled cigarettes and pipe Mn. lbs.	Chewing tobacco Mn. lbs.	Snuff Mn. lbs.	Total Mn. lbs.	Population Total Mns.	Population 15+ Mns.	Consumption per adult Cigarettes Number	Total Lbs.
1920	44,656	98·5	8,609	160·1	363·7		36·1	658·4	106·5	72·7	610	9·1
1921	50,899	112·2	7,435	138·3	350·8		35·7	637·0	108·5	74·1	690	8·6
1922	53,582	118·1	7,527	140·0	382·1		38·2	678·4	110·1	75·3	710	9·0
1923	64,469	142·2	7,505	139·6	372·7		39·4	693·9	111·9	76·7	840	9·0
1924	71,024	156·6	7,189	133·7	374·0		39·0	703·3	114·1	78·5	900	9·0
1925	79,976	176·3	6,949	129·3	372·4		37·8	715·8	115·8	79·9	1,000	9·0
1926	89,460	197·3	7,008	130·3	372·0		38·1	737·7	117·4	81·3	1,100	9·1
1927	97,188	214·3	7,008	130·3	353·9		40·2	738·7	119·0	82·7	1,180	8·9
1928	105,927	233·6	6,874	127·9	343·5		40·7	745·7	120·5	84·2	1,260	8·9
1929	119,049	262·5	6,972	129·7	337·7		40·0	769·9	121·8	85·6	1,390	9·0
1930	119,632	263·8	6,272	116·7	328·8		40·1	749·4	123·1	87·1	1,370	8·6
1931	113,455	250·2	5,656	105·2	328·0		39·5	722·9	124·0	88·2	1,290	8·2
1932	103,589	228·4	4,724	87·9	312·3		36·4	665·0	124·8	89·3	1,160	7·4
1933	111,766	246·4	4,553	84·7	304·9		36·3	672·3	125·6	90·5	1,230	7·4
1934	125,700	277·2	4,818	89·6	307·1		37·2	711·1	126·4	91·7	1,370	7·8
1935	134,610	296·8	4,943	91·9	304·3		38·1	729·1	127·3	92·9	1,450	7·8
1936	153,169	337·7	5,362	99·7	309·6		36·1	785·1	128·1	94·1	1,630	8·3
1937	162,629	358·6	5,516	102·6	300·9		36·9	799·0	128·8	95·2	1,710	8·4
1938	163,761	361·1	5,294	98·5	305·9		37·3	802·8	129·8	96·5	1,700	8·3
1939	172,469	380·3	5,469	101·7	302·8		38·0	822·8	130·9	97·8	1,760	8·4

Calendar year	Cigarettes Millions	Cigarettes Mn. lbs.	Cigars including little cigars Millions	Cigars Mn. lbs.	Tobacco for hand-rolled cigarettes and pipe Mn. lbs.	Chewing tobacco Mn. lbs.	Snuff Mn. lbs.	Total Mn. lbs.	Population Total Mns.	Population 15+ Mns.	Consumption per adult Cigarettes Number	Consumption per adult Total Lbs.
1940	180,664	398·4	5,491	102·1	304·3		37·9	842·7	132·0	99·0	1,820	8·5
1941	206,432	455·2	5,933	110·4	298·7		39·6	903·9	133·2	100·2	2,060	9·0
1942	235,841	520·0	6,339	117·9	280·5		41·2	959·6	134·7	101·4	2,330	9·5
1943	257,743	568·3	5,350	99·5	262·5		43·2	973·5	136·5	102·5	2,510	9·5
1944	239,287	527·6	4,878	90·7	251·8		42·0	912·1	138·1	103·5	2,310	8·8
1945	267,652	590·2	5,027	93·5	270·2		43·6	997·5	139·6	104·5	2,560	9·5
1946	321,475	708·9	5,929	110·3	211·1		39·7	1,070·0	141·4	105·3*	3,050	10·2
1947	335,965	740·1	5,706	106·1	199·2		39·3	1,084·7	144·1	106·8	3,150	10·2
1948	348,731	769·0	5,860	109·0	199·7		41·4	1,119·1	146·6	107·8*	3,230	10·4
1949	351,809	775·7	5,625	104·6	105·8	87·5	41·0	1,114·6	149·2	108·8	3,230	10·2
1950	360,199	794·2	5,608	104·3	104·3	85·9	40·0	1,128·7	152·3	111·3*	3,240	10·1
1951	379,725	837·3	5,778	107·5	97·4	84·3	39·2	1,165·7	154·9	112·5*	3,380	10·4
1952	394,109	908·4	6,037	112·3	92·9	82·8	38·8	1,235·2	157·5	113·5*	3,470	10·9
1953	386,826	902·9	6,107	113·6	84·3	82·0	38·9	1,221·7	160·2	114·6*	3,380	10·7
1954	368,725	865·0	6,024	112·0	81·2	79·3	38·6	1,176·1	163·0	115·8*	3,180	10·2
1955	382,061	894·8	6,078	113·1	77·8	77·5	39·0	1,202·2	165·9	116·9*	3,270	10·3
1956	393,154	916·0	6,039	112·3	70·0	74·2	37·6	1,210·1	168·9	118·2*	3,330	10·2
1957	409,436	922·5	6,194	115·2	68·9	70·8	36·1	1,213·5	172·0	119·6*	3,420	10·1
1958	436,354	961·3	6,586	118·5	74·4	68·0	34·8	1,257·0	174·9	121·2*	3,600	10·4
1959	453,681	983·7	7,377	132·8	71·9	66·7	33·6	1,288·7	177·8	122·7*	3,700	10·5

U.S.A. (contd)

Calendar year	Cigarettes Millions	Cigarettes Mn. lbs.	Cigars including little cigars — Large cigars Millions	Mn. lbs.	Little cigars Millions	lbs.	Tobacco for hand-rolled cigarettes and pipe Mn. lbs.	Chewing tobacco Mn. lbs.	Snuff Mn. lbs.	Total Mn. lbs.	Population Total Mns.	15+ Mns.	Consumption per adult Cigarettes Number	Total Lbs.
1960	470,136	998·3	7,097	127·7			72·2	63·8	34·7	1,296·7	180·7	124·3*	3,780	10·4
1961	488,119	1,050·5	7,083	127·5			72·7	64·4	33·7	1,348·8	183·8	126·1*	3,870	10·7
1962	494,463	1,047·3	7,103	127·9			69·8	63·8	33·1	1,341·9	186·5	128·4*	3,850	10·5
1963	509,588	1,137·0	7,434	133·8			69·7	64·5	31·9	1,436·9	189·2	130·4*	3,910	11·0
1964	497,447	1,093·0	8,959	156·8	940	2·4	81·7	65·5	31·3	1,430·7	191·9	132·5*	3,750	10·8
1965	511,464	1,125·0	8,514	149·0	435	1·1	69·8	63·9	29·5	1,438·3	194·3	134·5*	3,800	10·7
1966	522,533	1,107·0	8,174	143·0	436	1·1	68·6	64·2	29·5	1,413·4	196·6	136·6*	3,830	10·3
1967	527,800	1,092·0	7,972	139·5	431	1·1	66·4	64·3	28·9	1,392·2	198·7	138·8*	3,800	10·0
1968	523,008	1,084·0	7,827	137·0	504	1·3	69·6	65·4	27·7	1,385·0	200·7	141·2*	3,700	9·8
1969	510,531	1,037·0	7,848	137·3	731	1·8	68·3	69·3	26·9	1,340·6	202·7	143·5*	3,560	9·3
1970	532,769	1,039·0	7,985	139·7	896	2·2	74·0	68·2	26·7	1,349·8	204·9	146·1*	3,650	9·2
1971	528,858	1,015·0	7,747	135·6	1,083	2·7	69·5	71·8	26·6	1,321·2	207·0	148·7*	3,560	8·9
1972	551,017	1,081·0	7,192	125·9	3,933	9·8	66·8	72·5	25·7	1,381·7	208·8	151·0*	3,650	9·2
1973	590,300	1,120·0	6,891	120·6	4,334	10·8	59·5	74·5	25·5	1,410·9	210·8*	153·5*	3,850	9·2

Notes

(a) Details of the number of cigarettes and cigars and of the weight of tobacco consumed were obtained from the following:

1920–35 1st Annual Report on Tobacco Statistics, May, 1937.
1936–73 Annual Reports on Tobacco Statistics.
These are published by the United States Department of Agriculture.

(b) Cigarettes were converted from number to weight using a factor of 2·205 lbs. per 1,000 up to 1951. Since that date allowance has been made for the increasing consumption of 'king' size, 'long' size, and filter-tipped cigarettes. Cigars were converted at a rate of 18·6 lbs. per 1,000 up to 1957 and at 18 lbs. per 1,000 from 1958–1963. From 1964 onwards the conversion factors used for large and little cigars were 17·5 lbs. per 1,000 and 2·5 lbs. per 1,000 respectively.

(c) The sources of the population figures were as follows:
1920–45 Historical Statistics of the United States, 1789–1945, published by the United States Department of Commerce.
1946–72 United Nations Monthly Bulletin of Statistics and United Nations Demographic Yearbook.

46. Venezuela

Year ended 30th September	Cigarettes Millions	Mn. lbs.	Other manufactured tobacco Mn. lbs.	Population Total Mns.	15+ Mns.	Consumption per adult Cigarettes Number
1964	8,454	18·6	...	8·4	4·6*	1,840
1965	9,031	19·9	...	8·7	4·8*	1,900
1966	9,672	21·3	...	9·0	4·9*	1,960
1967	10,235	22·6	...	9·4	5·1*	2,000
1968	10,363	22·9	...	9·7	5·3*	1,960
1969	10,799	23·8	...	10·0	5·5*	1,970
1970	11,428	25·2	...	10·4	5·7*	2,000
1971	11,922	26·3	...	10·7	5·9	2,030
1972	12,848	28·3	...	11·2	6·1*	2,100
1973	14,068	31·0	...	11·6	6·4*	2,210

Notes

(a) Details of the number of cigarettes consumed were obtained from trade sources.

(b) Reliable statistics of the consumption of other manufactured tobacco products namely, cigars, cigarillos, cut tobacco, plug tobacco and pipe tobacco are not available.

(c) Cigarette consumption in pounds weight has been estimated from the number of cigarettes consumed by using a conversion factor of 2·205 lbs. per 1,000.

(d) Population figures were obtained from the General Statistics and Census Office of the Venezuelan Ministry of Development.

TOBACCO RESEARCH COUNCIL

RESEARCH PAPERS

No. 1. *Statistics of Smoking in the United Kingdom.* Edited by G. F. Todd. 6th edition, 1972.

No. 2. *The Reliability of Statements about Smoking Habits.* G. F. Todd and J. T. Laws. 2nd edition, 1959. (Out of print.) No. 2A. *Supplementary Report.* G. F. Todd, 1966.

No. 3. *The Constituents of Tobacco Smoke: An Annotated Bibliography.* Edited by H. R. Bentley and E. G. N. Berry, 1959. 1st Supplement, 1960. 2nd Supplement, 1963.

No. 4. *Cigarette Smoke Condensate: Preparation and Routine Laboratory Estimation.* H. R. Bentley and J. G. Burgan. 2nd edition, 1961. (Out of print.)

No. 5. *Cigarette Smoking Characteristics in the U.K., South Africa and Australia.* Edited by G. F. Todd, 1963.

No. 6. *Tobacco Consumption in Various Countries.* Edited by G. F. Todd, 1963. 4th edition, edited by P. N. Lee, 1975.

No. 7. *Mortality from Lung Cancer and Bronchitis in relation to Smoke and Sulphur Dioxide Concentration, Population Density and Social Index.* S. F. Buck and D. A. Brown, 1964.

No. 8. *Report on a Study of Environmental Factors Associated with Lung Cancer and Bronchitis Mortality in Areas of North-East England.* A. J. Wicken and S. F. Buck, 1964.

No. 9. *Environmental and Personal Factors in Lung Cancer and Bronchitis Mortality in Northern Ireland, 1960–62.* A. J. Wicken, 1966.

No. 10. *The Psychological Dynamics of Smoking.* F. E. Emery, E. Linden Hilgendorf and B. L. Irving, 1968. (Out of print.)

No. 11. *Standard Methods for the Analysis of Tobacco Smoke.* Compiled and edited by K. Rothwell and C. A. Grant. 2nd edition, 1974.

No. 12. *A Comparison of Two Smoking Typologies.* A. C. McKennell, 1973.

OCCASIONAL PAPERS

No. 1. *Changes in Smoking Patterns in the U.K.* G. F. Todd, 1975.

Available from
TOBACCO RESEARCH COUNCIL
Glen House, Stag Place, London SW1E 5AG
Telephone: 01-828 2041